Vasubandhu's Treatise
on
The Bodhisattva Vow

The publication of this book has been enabled by
a generous donation from Upāsaka Guo Ke.

A Note on the Proper Care of Dharma Materials

Traditional Buddhist cultures treat books on Dharma as sacred. Hence it is considered disrespectful to place them in a low position, to read them when lying down, or to place them where they might be damaged by food or drink.

Vasubandhu's Treatise on The Bodhisattva Vow

*A Discourse on the Bodhisattva's Vow
And the Practices Leading to Buddhahood*

Treatise On
The Generating the Bodhi Resolve Sutra

By Vasubandhu Bodhisattva
(*ca* 300 CE)

Translation by Bhikshu Dharmamitra

Kalavinka Press
Seattle, Washington
WWW.KALAVINKAPRESS.ORG

KALAVINKA PRESS
8603 39th Ave SW
Seattle, WA 98136 USA

WWW.KALAVINKAPRESS.ORG / WWW.KALAVINKA.ORG

Kalavinka Press is associated with the Kalavinka Dharma Association, a non-profit organized exclusively for religious educational purposes as allowed within the meaning of section 501(c)3 of the Internal Revenue Code. Kalavinka Dharma Association was founded in 1990 and gained formal approval in 2004 by the United States Internal Revenue Service as a 501(c)3 non-profit organization to which all donations are tax deductible.

Donations to KDA are accepted by mail and on the Kalavinka website where numerous free Dharma translations and excerpts from Kalavinka publications are available in digital format.

Edition: VBcitta-SA-1008-1.0
© 2005–2008 Bhikshu Dharmamitra
ISBN: 978-1-935413-09-7
Library of Congress Control Number: 2009920877

PUBLISHER'S CATALOGING-IN-PUBLICATION DATA

Vasubandhu, *ca* 300 ce

[Fa puti xin jing lun. English translation.]
Vasubandhu's Treatise on the Bodhisattva Vow. A Discourse on the Bodhisattva's Vow and the Practices Leading to Buddhahood.

Translated by Bhikshu Dharmamitra. – 1st ed. – Seattle, WA: Kalavinka Press, 2009.

p. ; cm.
ISBN: 978-1-935413-09-7
Includes: Text outline; facing-page Chinese source text in both traditional and simplified scripts; notes.

1. Bodhicitta (Buddhism). 2. Compassion—Religious aspects—Buddhism. 3. Bodhisattvas. 4. Spiritual life —Mahayana Buddhism. I. Title

2009920877
0902

Cover and interior designed and composed by Bhikshu Dharmamitra.

Dedicated to the memory of the selfless and marvelous life of the
Venerable Dhyāna Master Hsuan Hua, the Weiyang Ch'an Patriarch
and the very personification of the Bodhisattva Path.

Dhyāna Master Hsuan Hua
宣化禪師
1918–1995

About the Chinese Text

This translation is supplemented by inclusion of Chinese source text on verso pages in both traditional and simplified scripts. Taisho-supplied variant readings from other editions are presented as Chinese endnotes.

This Chinese text and its variant readings are from the Chinese Buddhist Electronic Text Association's digital edition of the Taisho compilation of the Buddhist canon.

Those following the translation in the Chinese should be aware that Taisho scripture punctuation is not traceable to original editions, is often erroneous and misleading, and is probably best ignored altogether. (In any case, accurate reading of Classical Chinese does not require any punctuation at all.)

Outlining in This Work

The twelve chapter titles in this work are from the Taisho Chinese text. All other outline headings originate with the translator. Buddhist canonical writings are often so metaphysically profound and structurally dense that they are best attended by detailed outline headings to facilitate understanding of the text.

Citation and Romanization Protocols

Kalavinka Press *Taisho* citation style adds text numbers after volume numbers and before page numbers to assist rapid digital searches. Romanization, where used, is Pinyin with the exception of names and terms already well-recognized in Wade-Giles romanization.

Contents

Vasubandhu's Treatise on the Bodhisattva Vow

About the Chinese Text	6
Outlining in This Work:	6
Citation and Romanization Protocols	6
Acknowledgments	12
The Translator's Introduction	13

Exhortation to Generate the Resolve — 17

I. Chapter 1: Exhortation to Generate the Resolve — 17
   A. Declaration of Reverence to the Buddhas — 17
   B. Introducing Bodhi Exhortation and the Practices Flowing Therefrom — 17
   C. The Practices Flowing from Exhortation to Resolve on Bodhi — 17
   D. The Rationale for Explaining These Dharmas — 19
   E. Praising Buddha's Qualities to Preserve the Buddhas' Lineage — 19
   F. The Immeasurable Practice of Those Resolved on Bodhi — 19
   G. The Incalculable Benefits Arising from Generating the Bodhi Resolve — 21
     1. Analogy: Like When the Great Sea Begins to Form — 21
     2. Analogy: Like When the Great Trichiliocosm Forms — 21
     3. Bodhi Resolve as Guided by Kindness and Compassion Immeasurables — 23
     4. Analogy: Bodhi Resolve Comparable in Inclusiveness to Empty Space — 23
     5. Analogy: Bodhi Resolve Equals in Vastness All Realms of Beings — 23
     6. Summation on Exhortation to Generate the Bodhi Resolve — 25

Generating the Resolve — 27

II. Chapter 2: Generating the Resolve — 27
   A. Ten Factors Conducing to Generation of the Bodhi resolve — 27
   B. Four Additional Bases for Generation of the Bodhi Resolve — 27
     1. Contemplation of All Buddhas — 29
     2. Contemplation of the Body's Faults and Perilous Aspects — 29
     3. Generating Resolve Based on Seeking the Path's Supreme Fruits — 31
     4. Generating the Bodhi resolve Based on Kindness and Pity — 33
       a. Observing that Beings Are Tied up by Ignorance — 33
       b. Observing that Beings Are Bound up by Manifold Sufferings — 33
       c. Observing that Beings Are Engaged in Accumulating Bad Karma — 35
       d. Observing that Beings Are Engaged in Extremely Grave Evils — 35
       e. Observing that Beings Fail to Cultivate Right Dharma — 37
   C. Summation on the Causal Bases for Generating the Bodhi resolve — 37

The Establishment of Vows — 39

III. Chapter 3: The Establishment of Vows — 39
- A. Introduction to the Bodhisattva's Establishment of Vows — 39
- B. The Ten Great Vows — 39
- C. The Six *Pāramitās* and Related Practices as Causes of Bodhi — 43
- D. The Importance of Refraining from Negligence — 45
- E. Making Definitely-Resolved Vows as Supporting Five Endeavors — 45
- F. The Buddha's Own Praise of the Unsurpassed Power of Vows — 45
- G. Establishing Six Resolutions in Support of the Six Perfections — 45
- H. The Importance of the Ten Vows and Six Resolutions to Bodhi — 47

Dāna Pāramitā — 51

IV. Chapter 4: The Perfection of Giving — 51
- A. Three Kinds of Benefit and Path Adornment Arising from Giving — 51
  1. Right Motivation in the Practice of Giving — 51
  2. Self-Benefit — 51
  3. Benefit of Others — 51
  4. Combined Benefit — 51
  5. Adorning the Path of Bodhi through Giving — 53
- B. The Three Types of Giving — 53
  1. The Giving of Dharma — 53
  2. The Giving of Fearlessness — 53
  3. The Definition and Scope of the Giving of Material Wealth — 53
     1) Five Subcategories of the Giving of Material Wealth — 53
     2) Five Categories of Wrong Giving — 55
     3) Summary of Wrong and Right Giving — 55
- C. Five Additional Benefits of Delighting in Giving — 55
- D. Universality in Giving, the Defining Characteristic of a Bodhisattva — 55
- E. Types of Giving as Bases for Corresponding Karmic Fruits — 57
- F. Summation on the Bodhisattva's Cultivation of Giving — 59
- G. The Essence of the Bodhisattva's Perfection of Giving — 59

Śīla Pāramitā — 61

V. Chapter 5: The Perfection of Moral Virtue — 61
- A. Three Kinds of Benefit and Path Adornment from Moral Virtue — 61
  1. Right Motivation in the Practice of Moral Virtue — 61
  2. Self Benefit — 61
  3. Benefit of Others — 61
  4. Combined Benefit — 61
  5. Adorning the Path of Bodhi through Moral Virtue — 61
- B. The Three Types of Moral Precepts — 63
  1. The Moral precepts Associated with the Body — 63
  2. The Moral precepts Associated with the Mouth — 63

3.	The Moral Precepts Associated with the Mind	65
4.	Five Benefits Arising from the Precepts of the Ten Good Karmas	65
5.	Summary Discussion of the Precepts of the Ten Good Karmas	65
C.	The Five Categories of Moral Precepts	67
D.	Rationales for Observing Precepts Linked to Specific Path Practices	67
E.	Factors Defining "Purity in Observing Moral Precepts"	69
F.	Summation on the Bodhisattva's Cultivation of Moral Purity	71
G.	The Essence of the Bodhisattva's Perfection of Moral Virtue	73

Kṣānti Pāramitā   75

VI. Chapter 6: The Perfection of Patience   75

- A. Three Kinds of Benefit and Path Adornment from Patience   75
  1. Right Motivation in the Practice of Patience   75
  2. Self Benefit   75
  3. Benefit of Others   75
  4. Combined Benefit   75
  5. Adorning the Path of Bodhi through Patience   75
- B. The Three Types of Patience   77
  1. Physical Patience   77
  2. Verbal Patience   77
  3. Mental Patience   77
- C. Two Types of Beatings   77
- D. Two Types of Scoldings   79
- E. The Necessity of Patience When Subjected to Others' Hatred   79
- F. Retributions Corresponding to Presence or Absence of Patience   81
- G. Ten Bases for Developing Patience   81
- H. Qualifications Prerequisite to Pure and Ultimate Patience   81
- I. Summation on the Bodhisattva's Cultivation of Patience   83
- J. The Essence of the Bodhisattva's Perfection of Patience   83

Vīrya Pāramitā   85

VII. Chapter 7: The Perfection of Vigor   85

- A. Three Kinds of Benefit and Path Adornment from Vigor   85
  1. Right Motivation in the Practice of Vigor   85
  2. Self-Benefit   85
  3. Benefit of Others   85
  4. Combined Benefit   85
  5. Adorning the Path of Bodhi through Vigor   85
- B. Two Types of Vigor   87
- C. Ten Recollections as Bases for Diligent Practice of Vigor   87
- D. The Four Right Efforts   89
- E. Practice Scenarios Exemplifying Vigor   89
- F. The Bodhisattva's Stately Deportment and Alignment with Dharma   91

G.	The Importance of Vigor to the *Pāramitās* and Buddhahood	91
H.	Four Factors in the Bodhisattva's Initiation of the Great Adornment	91
	1. The Initiation of the Great Adornment	93
	2. The Accumulation of Heroic Strength	93
	3. The Cultivation of Roots of Goodness	93
	4. The Teaching and Transforming of Beings	93
I.	Summation on Vigor	93
J.	The Essence of the Bodhisattva's Perfection of Vigor	95

Dhyāna Pāramitā   97

VIII. Chapter 8: The Perfection of Dhyāna Meditation   97

- A. Three Kinds of Benefit and Path Adornment from Dhyāna   97
  1. Right Motivation in the Practice of Dhyāna   97
  2. Self-Benefit   97
  3. Benefit of Others   97
  4. Combined Benefit   97
  5. Adorning the Path of Bodhi through Dhyāna   99
- B. The Three Dharmas from which Dhyāna Absorption Arises   99
  1. Learning-Derived Wisdom   99
  2. Deliberation-Derived Wisdom   99
  3. Meditation-Derived Wisdom   101
  4. Summation on the Three Types of Wisdom from Dhyāna   103
- C. Ten Meditation Dharmas Not in Common with the Two Vehicles   103
- D. Additional Characteristics of Bodhisattva Meditation Practice   107
- E. Four Additional Distinctive Factors in Bodhisattva Meditation   107
  1. Spiritual Penetrations   107
  2. Knowing Awareness   107
  3. Skillful Means   109
  4. Wisdom   109
- F. Summation on the Bodhisattva's Distinctive Meditation Practice   109
- G. The Essence of the Bodhisattva's Perfection of Dhyāna Meditation   109

Prajñā Pāramitā   111

IX. Chapter 9: The Perfection of Wisdom   111

- A. Three Kinds of Benefit and Path Adornment from Wisdom   111
  1. Right Motivation in the Practice of Wisdom   111
  2. Self-Benefit   111
  3. Benefit of Others   111
  4. Combined Benefit   111
  5. Adorning the Path of Bodhi through Wisdom   111
- B. Twenty Types of Mind Key to a Bodhisattva's Wisdom Realization   113
- C. Ten Dharmas of Skillful Contemplation Exclusive to Bodhisattvas   115
- D. The Bodhisattva's Twelve-fold Skillful Entry of Dharma Gateways   117

E.	The Bodhisattva's Contemplation of the Three Periods of Time	119
F.	Summation on the Bodhisattva's Wisdom-Based Contemplation	119
G.	The Essence of the Bodhisattva's Perfection of Wisdom	121

The Dharma Gateway of Accordance with Reality 123

X. Chapter 10: The Dharma Gateway of Accordance with Reality 123

- A. Seven Dharmas to be Abandoned 123
- B. Seven Dharmas to be Cultivated 125
- C. Bodhi Resolve's Incompatibility with "Something to be Gained" 127
- D. Generation of Bodhi Resolve and Contemplation of Emptiness 127
- E. The Practice of the Bodhisattva Who Understands Emptiness 129
- F. The Fruits of this Bodhisattva Practice 129

Emptiness and Signlessness 131

XI. Chapter 11: Emptiness and Signlessness 131

- A. An Introductory Passage from Scripture: 131
  1. Explanation of the Concepts of "Emptiness" and "Signlessness" 131
  2. A Comprehensive Analogy 133
- B. Faith-Based Patience and its Role in Realizing Fruits of the Path 137
- C. Acquiescence-Based Patience from Partial Cognition of Non-Self 139
- D. Supreme Patience via Faith-Based and Acquiescence-Based Patience 139

On the Merit and on Preserving Dharma 141

XII. Chapter 12: On the Merit and on Preserving Dharma 141

- A. Characteristics of a Bodhisattva's Bodhi-Directed Cultivation 141
- B. Ten Bodhisattva Dharmas Ensuring Non-Retreat 141
- C. Benefits Arising from Scriptures Such as These 143
- D. The Meritoriousness of this Sutra and Those Revering It 145

Endnotes 149
Variant Readings from Other Chinese Editions 153
About the Translator 157
Kalavinka Buddhist Classics Title List 159

Acknowledgments

The accuracy and readability of these first ten books of translations have been significantly improved with the aid of extensive corrections, preview comments, and editorial suggestions generously contributed by Bhikkhu Bodhi, Jon Babcock, Timothy J. Lenz, Upāsaka Feng Ling, Upāsaka Guo Ke, Upāsikā Min Li, and Richard Robinson. Additional valuable editorial suggestions and corrections were offered by Bhikshu Huifeng, and Bruce Munson.

The publication of the initial set of ten translation volumes has been assisted by substantial donations to the Kalavinka Dharma Association by Bill and Peggy Brevoort, Freda Chen, David Fox, Upāsaka Guo Ke, Chenping and Luther Liu, Sunny Lou, Jimi Neal, and "Leo L." (a.k.a. *Camellia sinensis folium*). Additional helpful donations were offered by Doug Adams, Diane Hodgman, Bhikshu Huifeng, Joel and Amy Lupro, Richard Robinson, Ching Smith, and Sally and Ian Timm.

Were it not for the ongoing material support provided by my late guru's Dharma Realm Buddhist Association and the serene translation studio provided by Seattle's Bodhi Dhamma Center, creation of this translation would have been immensely more difficult.

Most importantly, it would have been impossible for me to produce this translation without the Dharma teachings provided by my late guru, the Weiyang Ch'an Patriarch, Dharma teacher, and exegete, the Venerable Master Hsuan Hua.

Translator's Introduction

I am pleased to be able to present here in English translation a marvelous treatise[1] by Vasubandhu Bodhisattva on the most crucial of all topics in Mahāyāna Buddhism, namely, the altruistic resolve on the part of the bodhisattva to gain the utmost, right, and perfect enlightenment of a buddha. Although there are numerous examples of primary and secondary works in the Mahāyāna canon focusing on the resolve to become a buddha, I have as yet found none which so completely and concisely distill into a short and potent work all of the metaphysical teachings and bodhisattva path practices most directly relevant to this most essential of bodhisattva vows.[2]

My keen interest in translating this work stems in part from an observation regarding the manner in which many students of Dharma respond to Buddhism as it is presented to them in Western Dharma communities. Understandably, practitioners tend to focus primarily upon meditation practice as a powerfully effective means for reducing personal afflictions and enhancing happiness. One of the consequences of this exclusive focus on maintaining a sense of personal well-being and peacefulness in the near term is that one may not concern oneself so much with the true character of the longer-term spiritual Path presented by the Buddha. As a result, it is common for meditation-focused Dharma students to remain oblivious to the significance and essentiality of the bodhisattva vow.

Having noticed this phenomenon, I have made a point of translating a range of authoritative works which teach meditation and doctrine in great detail, but which do so only in the context of the greater vision of what comprises the means to spiritual liberation in the Buddhist path. Among these translations are four works on the topic of *bodhicitta*, the bodhisattva's resolve to become a buddha. The most doctrinally-specific and practice-specific of those *bodhicitta*-focused works is the present work authored by Vasubandhu. The other three texts (by Ārya Nāgārjuna, Patriarch Sheng'an Shixian, and the Tang Dynasty literatus, Peixiu) are published under separate cover as *On Generating the Resolve to Become a Buddha*. I hope that translation of these bodhi-resolve texts may make some small contribution to the development of a more nuanced understanding of Mahāyāna Buddhism among Western Buddhists.

The author of *Treatise on the Generating the Bodhi Resolve Sutra* is the justifiably famous scholar-monk and incredibly prolific treatise-master, Vasubandhu, about whom much has already been written in translations and secondary works by secular buddhologists. As with many matters in secular buddhology, there is no consensus on the precise dates of Vasubandhu. My own view on the issue, imprecise as it is, finds that the currently dominant scholarly opinion seems to place the time of Vasubandhu's flourishing too late to explain how Kumārjīva would have translated this work as early as he did. It is primarily for this reason that I estimate Vasubandhu most likely flourished not too much later than 300 CE.

Vasubandhu is famous not only for being an author of many commentaries and treatises, but also for being a late-in-life convert to the Mahāyāna who was inspired to this doctrinal shift by his equally-famous treatise-master brother, Asaṅga. Vasubandhu's writings on the Great Vehicle were so compelling that the Chinese Buddhist tradition universally refers to him as "Vasubandhu Bodhisattva."

I should mention that the twelve chapter titles in this work originate with the text itself, for they are not only printed at the beginning of each chapter, but are also listed in precise order, but more expansively, within the very first paragraphs of Vasubandhu's treatise. All additional outline headings originate with the English translator's attempt to make this doctrinally complex text more easily intelligible. I do not claim in this outlining to have perfectly captured the architecture of Vasubandhu's treatise, but do nonetheless feel the attempt will serve the reader's access to the text.

I will conclude this short translator's introduction by mentioning that there is an unresolved question as to which sutra is referenced by Vasubandhu in this *Treatise on the Generating the Bodhi Resolve Sutra*. I performed multiple digital searches in the Chinese Buddhist Canon on passages deduced by textual analysis to be fragments of sutra text commented upon by Vasubandhu, yet failed to find definitely positive correlations. As it turns out, this is probably of little or no consequence. Vasubandhu's text remains as a free-standing discourse which, on its own, completely explores the significance and praxis implications of the resolve to become a buddha.

I hope that readers may find inspiration in Vasubandhu's treatise on the bodhisattva's resolve.

Bhikshu Dharmamitra
Seattle
November 1, 2008

A Treatise On
The Generating the Bodhi Resolve Sutra

By Vasubandhu Bodhisattva
(*ca* 300 CE)

Chinese Translation by Tripiṭaka Master Kumārajīva
(344–413 CE)

English Translation by Bhikshu Dharmamitra

No. 1659

發菩提心[p508n01]經論卷上。

[2]天親菩薩造。

[3]後秦龜茲國三藏鳩摩羅什譯。

勸發品第一。

敬禮無邊際。去來現在佛。
等空不動智。救世大悲尊。

[0508c12] 有大方等最上妙法。摩得勒伽藏菩薩摩訶薩之所修行。所謂勸樂修集無上菩提。能令眾生發深廣心。建立誓願畢定莊嚴。捨身命財攝伏貪恪。修五聚戒化導犯禁。行畢竟[4]忍調伏瞋[5]礙發勇精進安止眾生。集諸禪定為知眾心。修行智慧滅除無明。入如實[6]門離諸執著。宣示甚深空無相行。稱讚功德使佛種不斷。

1
Exhortation to Generate the Resolve

I. CHAPTER 1: EXHORTATION TO GENERATE THE RESOLVE
   A. DECLARATION OF REVERENCE TO THE BUDDHAS

I respectfully pay reverence to the boundless community
Of past, future, and present-era Buddhas,
The possessors of unshakable wisdom as vast as space,
The saviors of worlds, the greatly compassionate Bhagavāns.

   B. INTRODUCING BODHI EXHORTATION AND THE PRACTICES FLOWING THEREFROM

There exists among the *mahāvaipulya*[3] teachings the most superior and sublime of dharmas. Drawn from the *mātṛkā*[4] treasury and cultivated by the Bodhisattvas and the Mahāsattvas, it is:

1. The exhortation to delight in cultivating and accumulating [the bases for realization of] the unsurpassed bodhi.[5]

   C. THE PRACTICES FLOWING FROM EXHORTATION TO RESOLVE ON BODHI

By resort to it, one is able to influence other beings:

2. To generate the profound and vast resolve;
3. To establish the vows to carry out the most definite form of adornment;[6]
4. To relinquish lives and wealth in subduing covetousness;
5. To cultivate the five groups of moral precepts, teaching and leading forth those transgressing against the prohibitions;
6. To practice the ultimate patience by which they control and subdue the hindrance of hatred;
7. To generate the heroic vigor through which they establish and stabilize beings;
8. To accumulate the dhyāna absorptions for the sake of knowing the minds of the many varieties of beings;
9. To cultivate wisdom, destroying and eliminating ignorance;
10. To enter the gateway of according with reality, thus abandoning all forms of attachment;
11. To propagate and explain the extremely profound practices of emptiness and signlessness;
12. And to proclaim praises of the associated merit, thus preventing the lineage of the Buddhas from being cut off.

有如是等无量方便助菩提法清净之门。当为一切上上善欲分别显示。悉令究竟阿耨多罗三藐三菩提。诸佛子。若佛[7]子受持佛语。能为众生演说法者。应先称扬佛之功德。众生闻已乃能发心求佛智慧。以发心故佛种不断。若比丘比丘尼优婆塞优婆夷。念佛念法又念如来。行菩萨道时为求法故。阿僧只劫受诸勤苦。以如是念。为菩萨说法乃至一偈。菩萨得闻是法示教利喜。当种善根修习佛法。得阿耨多罗三藐三菩提。为断无量众生无始生死诸苦恼故。菩萨摩诃萨欲成无量身心。勤修精进深发大愿。行大方便起大慈悲。求大智慧无见顶相。求如是等诸佛大法。当知是法无量无边。法无量故福德果报亦复无量。

简体字

有如是等無量方便助菩提法清淨之門。當為一切上上善欲分別顯示。悉令究竟阿耨多羅三藐三菩提。諸佛子。若佛[7]子受持佛語。能為眾生演說法者。應先稱揚佛之功德。眾生聞已乃能發心求佛智慧。以發心故佛種不斷。若比丘比丘尼優婆塞優婆夷。念佛念法又念如來。行菩薩道時為求法故。阿僧祇劫受諸勤苦。以如是念。為菩薩說法乃至一偈。菩薩得聞是法示教利喜。當種善根修習佛法。得阿耨多羅三藐三菩提。為斷無量眾生無始生死諸苦惱故。菩薩摩訶薩欲成無量身心。勤修精進深發大願。行大方便起大慈悲。求大智慧無見頂相。求如是等諸佛大法。當知是法無量無邊。法無量故福德果報亦復無量。

正體字

D. THE RATIONALE FOR EXPLAINING THESE DHARMAS

There are countless skillful means such as these which serve as dharmas assisting bodhi (*bodhipakṣa dharma*) and which serve as gateways associated with purification. These should be distinguished and explained for all who possess the most supremely excellent aspiration, thus allowing them to gain complete realization of *anuttara-samyak-saṃbodhi*.

E. PRAISING BUDDHA'S QUALITIES TO PRESERVE THE BUDDHAS' LINEAGE

"Sons of the Buddha, if a son of the Buddha accepts and upholds the discourses of the Buddha and is able to expound the Dharma for the sake of beings, he should first proclaim and make known the meritorious qualities of the Buddha." Once beings have heard this, they then become able to generate the resolve to seek the wisdom of the Buddha. It is on account of this generation of the resolve that severance of the lineage of the Buddhas is prevented.

When bhikshus, bhikshunis, *upāsakas*, or *upāsikās* practice mindfulness of the Buddha and mindfulness of the Dharma, they also bring to mind the *asaṃkhyeya* kalpas the Tathāgata spent cultivating the Bodhisattva Path, enduring all manner of intense suffering while seeking the Dharma. If on account of cultivating such mindfulness they were then to explain so much as a single verse of Dharma for the sake of some bodhisattva and that bodhisattva were to hear the teaching of this Dharma and were to thereby be benefited and delighted by it—this would result in his planting roots of goodness, in his cultivating the Dharma of the Buddha, and in his ultimately realizing *anuttara-samyak-saṃbodhi*.

F. THE IMMEASURABLE PRACTICE OF THOSE RESOLVED ON BODHI

For the sake of cutting off the sufferings and afflictions besetting the countless beings coursing in the beginningless round of births and deaths, bodhisattvas and *mahāsattvas* strive to perfect immeasurability in their manifestations of body and mind. They diligently cultivate vigor and, with deep resolve, generate great vows. They implement great skillful means and bring forth the great kindness and the great compassion. They seek to gain the great wisdom and the vision-surpassing summit mark.[7] They seek to acquire all of the great dharmas of a buddha such as these. One should realize that these dharmas are themselves immeasurable and boundless. Because these dharmas are immeasurable, the karmic blessings resulting from them are also immeasurable.

如来说言如诸菩萨最初发心下劣一念福德果报。百千万劫说不能尽。况复一日一月一岁乃至百岁。所习诸心福德果报岂可说尽。何以故。菩萨所行无尽。欲令一切众生皆住无生法忍。得阿耨多罗三藐三菩提故。诸佛子。菩萨初始发菩提心。譬如大海初渐起时。当知皆为下中上价乃至无价如意宝珠作所住处。此宝皆从大海生故。菩萨发心亦复如是。初渐起时。当知便为人天声闻缘觉[p509n01]诸佛菩萨一切善法禅定智慧之所生处。复次又如三千大千世界初渐起时。当知便为二十五有。其中所有一切众生。悉皆荷负作依止处。菩萨发菩提心亦复如是。初渐起时。普为一切无量众生。所谓六趣四生。正见邪见修善习恶。护持净戒犯四重禁。尊奉三宝谤毁正法。

简体字

如來說言如諸菩薩最初發心下劣一念福德果報。百千萬劫說不能盡。況復一日一月一歲乃至百歲。所習諸心福德果報豈可說盡。何以故。菩薩所行無盡。欲令一切眾生皆住無生法忍。得阿耨多羅三藐三菩提故。諸佛子。菩薩初始發菩提心。譬如大海初漸起時。當知皆為下中上價乃至無價如意寶珠作所住處。此寶皆從大海生故。菩薩發心亦復如是。初漸起時。當知便為人天聲聞緣覺[p509n01]諸佛菩薩一切善法禪定智慧之所生處。復次又如三千大千世界初漸起時。當知便為二十五有。其中所有一切眾生。悉皆荷負作依止處。菩薩發菩提心亦復如是。初漸起時。普為一切無量眾生。所謂六趣四生。正見邪見修善習惡。護持淨戒犯四重禁。尊奉三寶謗毀正法。

正體字

Chapter 1: *Exhortation to Generate the Resolve*

G. The Incalculable Benefits Arising from Generating the Bodhi Resolve

The Tathāgata stated, for instance, that the karmic blessings resulting from even the lowliest and most feeble single initial thought of a bodhisattva "generating the resolve" are such that they could not be completely described even in a hundred thousand myriads of kalpas. How much the less could the resultant karmic blessings be completely described where one has coursed in such thoughts of resolve for a day, a month, a year, or even a hundred years?

Why is this the case? Whatsoever is practiced by a bodhisattva is itself endless. He desires to cause all beings to abide in the unproduced-dharmas patience and then succeed in realizing *anuttara-samyak-saṃbodhi*.

1. Analogy: Like When the Great Sea Begins to Form

Sons of the Buddha, when the bodhisattva first brings forth the bodhi resolve, it is analogous to when the great sea first gradually begins to rise into existence. One should realize that it then becomes the abiding place for all of the lesser-value, middling-value, superior-value, and priceless "as-you-wish-it" wishing pearls, this because all of these jewels are born from within the great sea.

When the bodhisattva generates the resolve, that circumstance is just the same. When [this nascent bodhi resolve] first gradually begins to rise into existence, one should realize that it then becomes the birthplace of all of the good dharmas, dhyāna absorptions, and wisdom possessed by humans, gods, śrāvaka-disciples, pratyeka-buddhas, buddhas, and bodhisattvas.

2. Analogy: Like When the Great Trichiliocosm Forms

Additionally, this is also comparable to when the great trichiliocosm first gradually rises into existence. One should realize that it then takes on the burden of all beings of the twenty-five realms of existence and becomes the place in which they abide.

When the bodhisattva generates the bodhi resolve, it is just the same as this. When it first gradually rises into existence, it then universally takes on the burden of all of the incalculably many beings and becomes for them that upon which they rely. This includes those of the six destinies and four types of birth, those possessed of right views and those possessed of perverse views, those who cultivate goodness and those who course in evil, those who guard and uphold the precepts of moral purity and those who transgress against the four serious monastic prohibitions, those who reverently esteem the Triple Jewel and those who slander right Dharma,

诸魔外道沙门梵志。刹利婆罗门毘舍首陀。一切荷负作依止处。复次菩萨发心。慈悲为首。菩萨[2]之慈[3]无边无量。是故发心无有齐限等众生界。譬如虚空无不普覆。菩萨发心亦复如是。一切众生无不覆者。如众生界无量无边不可穷尽。菩萨发心亦复如是。无量无边无有穷尽。虚空无尽故众生无尽。众生无尽故菩萨发心等众生界。众生界者无有齐限。我今当承圣旨说其少分。东方尽千亿恒河沙阿僧只诸佛世界。南西北方四维上下各千亿恒河沙阿僧只诸佛世界。尽末为[4]尘。此诸微尘皆不与肉眼作对。百万亿恒河沙阿僧只三千大千世界所有众生。悉共聚集共取一尘。二百万亿恒河沙阿僧只三千大千世界所有众生。共取二尘。

简体字

諸魔外道沙門梵志。刹利婆羅門毘舍首陀。一切荷負作依止處。復次菩薩發心。慈悲為首。菩薩[2]之慈[3]無邊無量。是故發心無有齊限等眾生界。譬如虛空無不普覆。菩薩發心亦復如是。一切眾生無不覆者。如眾生界無量無邊不可窮盡。菩薩發心亦復如是。無量無邊無有窮盡。虛空無盡故眾生無盡。眾生無盡故菩薩發心等眾生界。眾生界者無有齊限。我今當承聖旨說其少分。東方盡千億恒河沙阿僧祇諸佛世界。南西北方四維上下各千億恒河沙阿僧祇諸佛世界。盡末為[4]塵。此諸微塵皆不與肉眼作對。百萬億恒河沙阿僧祇三千大千世界所有眾生。悉共聚集共取一塵。二百萬億恒河沙阿僧祇三千大千世界所有眾生。共取二塵。

正體字

Chapter 1: *Exhortation to Generate the Resolve* 23

and those who are demons, non-Buddhists, śramaṇas, *brahmacārins*, *kṣatriyas*, brahmins, *vaiśyas*, and *śūdras*.

3. Bodhi Resolve as Guided by Kindness and Compassion Immeasurables

Additionally, when the bodhisattva generates the resolve, it is kindness and compassion which are taken as foremost. The bodhisattva's kindness is boundless and immeasurable. Therefore this generation of the resolve is itself free of any boundaries and is equal in its vastness to the expansiveness of all of the realms inhabited by beings.

4. Analogy: Bodhi Resolve Comparable in Inclusiveness to Empty Space

This is comparable to empty space, for there is nothing which is not universally embraced by it. When the bodhisattva generates the resolve, it is just the same. Of all of the beings, there are none who are not embraced by it. Just as the realms of beings are incalculably many, boundless, and endless, so too it is with the bodhisattva's generation of the resolve. It is incalculably vast, boundless, and endless.

5. Analogy: Bodhi Resolve Equals in Vastness All Realms of Beings

Because empty space is endless, beings, too, are endless. Because beings are endless, the bodhisattva's generation of the resolve is equivalent in its vastness to the realms of beings.

As for "the realms of beings," they have no boundaries. I should now take up the intent of the Āryas in this regard and discuss a minor measure of it:

Suppose that one were to take from the easterly direction a thousand *koṭīs* of Ganges' sands of *asaṃkhyeyas* of buddhalands while also taking a thousand *koṭīs* of Ganges' sands of *asaṃkhyeyas* of buddhalands from each of the other directions, from the southerly, westerly, and northerly directions, from the four intermediary directions, from the zenith, and from the nadir. Now suppose that one were to then grind them all into dust motes so fine that they could not be seen by the naked fleshly eye.

Now suppose again that one were to remove just a single one of these dust motes as a signifier to represent an aggregation of all of the beings from the worlds contained in a hundred myriads of *koṭīs* of Ganges' sands of *asaṃkhyeyas* of great trichiliocosms. Then suppose that one then removed a second one of these dust motes as a signifier to represent a second aggregated group of all of the beings contained in the worlds contained in another hundred myriads of *koṭīs* of Ganges' sands of *asaṃkhyeyas* of great trichiliocosms.

简体字	正體字
如是展转取十方各千亿恒河沙阿僧只诸佛世界所有地种。微尘都尽。是众生界犹不可尽。譬如有人析破一毛以为百分。以一分毛[5]渧大海水。我今所说众生少分亦复如是。其不说者如大海水。假使诸佛于无量无边阿僧只劫。广演譬喻说亦不尽。菩萨发心悉能遍覆如是众生。云何诸佛子。是菩提心岂可尽也。若有菩萨闻如是说。不惊不怖不退不没。当知是人决定能发菩提之心。假令无量一切诸佛于无量阿僧只劫。赞其功德亦不可尽。何以故。是菩提心无有齐限不可尽故。有如是等无量利益。是故宣说为令众生普[6]得受行。发菩提心。	如是展轉取十方各千億恒河沙阿僧祇諸佛世界所有地種。微塵都盡。是眾生界猶不可盡。譬如有人析破一毛以為百分。以一分毛[5]渧大海水。我今所說眾生少分亦復如是。其不說者如大海水。假使諸佛於無量無邊阿僧祇劫。廣演譬喻說亦不盡。菩薩發心悉能遍覆如是眾生。云何諸佛子。是菩提心豈可盡也。若有菩薩聞如是說。不驚不怖不退不沒。當知是人決定能發菩提之心。假令無量一切諸佛於無量阿僧祇劫。讚其功德亦不可盡。何以故。是菩提心無有齊限不可盡故。有如是等無量利益。是故宣說為令眾生普[6]得受行。發菩提心。

Finally, suppose that one proceeded in sequential manner with this calculation until one had removed all of those fine dust motes contained in the earth element in a thousand *koṭīs* of Ganges' sands of *asaṃkhyeyas* of buddhalands in each of the ten directions. In such a case, one would still not have come to the end of all of these "realms of beings."

Now suppose that there was a person who split a single hair into a hundred filaments and then, by dipping one of them into the water, drew forth a droplet of the great sea's waters. The minor portion of all beings which I have just now described would be comparable only to this whereas those beings not subsumed within that description would be comparable to all of the waters remaining in the great sea. Beings are so numerous that, even if all buddhas discoursed on the matter for an incalculable and boundless number of *asaṃkhyeyas* of kalpas, resorting to extensive expounding of analogies, they still would not completely include them all.

When the bodhisattva generates the resolve, it is able to completely extend to all of these beings. Sons of the Buddha, how then could one be able to reach the end of this bodhi resolve's vastness?

6. Summation on Exhortation to Generate the Bodhi Resolve

If there are bodhisattvas who hear this description and yet are not frightened by it, who are not struck with terror by it, and who are not caused to retreat and sink away by it, then one should realize that these persons are definitely able to generate the bodhi resolve. Even if all of the incalculably many buddhas praised the merit of such a person for an incalculable number of *asaṃkhyeyas* of kalpas, they still would not be able to completely describe it. Why is this the case? It is because this bodhi resolve is itself boundless and is such as one cannot come to the end of. It is because it possesses such an incalculable measure of benefits that these qualities are proclaimed. This is done for the sake of influencing all beings to universally embrace it in practice and thus initiate their own resolve to realize bodhi.

[7]发菩提心[8]经论。

发心品第二。

[0509b20] 菩萨云何发菩提心。以何因缘修集菩提。若菩萨亲近善知识供养诸佛。修集善根志求[9]胜法。心常柔和遭苦能忍。慈悲淳厚深心平等。信乐大乘求佛智慧。若人能具如是十法。乃能发阿耨多罗三藐三菩提心。复有四缘。发心[10]修集无上菩提。何谓为四。一者思惟诸佛发菩提心。二者观身过患发菩提心。三者慈愍众生发菩提心。四者求最胜果发菩提心。

简体字

[7]發菩提心[8]經論。

發心品第二。

[0509b20] 菩薩云何發菩提心。以何因緣修集菩提。若菩薩親近善知識供養諸佛。修集善根志求[9]勝法。心常柔和遭苦能忍。慈悲淳厚深心平等。信樂大乘求佛智慧。若人能具如是十法。乃能發阿耨多羅三藐三菩提心。復有四緣。發心[10]修集無上菩提。何謂為四。一者思惟諸佛發菩提心。二者觀身過患發菩提心。三者慈愍眾生發菩提心。四者求最勝果發菩提心。

正體字

2
Generating the Resolve

II. CHAPTER 2: GENERATING THE RESOLVE

How does the bodhisattva generate the bodhi resolve? Relying on what sort of causes and conditions does one cultivate and accumulate the bases for realizing bodhi?

A. TEN FACTORS CONDUCING TO GENERATION OF THE BODHI RESOLVE

[Those causal bases are present] in a case where a bodhisattva:

1. Draws close to a good spiritual guide;
2. Makes offerings to the Buddhas;
3. Cultivates and accumulates roots of goodness;
4. Resolves to seek the supreme Dharma;
5. Maintains constant pliancy and harmoniousness of mind;
6. On encountering suffering, remains able to endure it;
7. Possesses pure and abundant kindness and compassion;
8. Maintains a profound mind dedicated to maintaining equal regard for all;
9. Possesses faith and happiness in the Great Vehicle; and
10. Seeks to gain the wisdom of the Buddha.

If a person is able to embody ten dharmas such as these, he will then become able to generate the mind resolved on realizing *anuttarasamyak-saṃbodhi*.

B. FOUR ADDITIONAL BASES FOR GENERATION OF THE BODHI RESOLVE

There are four additional conditions which may be involved in generating the resolve to cultivate and accumulate the bases for realization of the unsurpassed bodhi. What are those four?

First, it may be based on contemplation of all buddhas that one generates the bodhi resolve.

Second, it may be based on contemplation of the faults and perilous aspects of the physical body that one generates the bodhi resolve.

Third, it may be that it is based on seeking the most supreme of all fruits [of the Path] that one generates the bodhi resolve.[8]

Fourth, it may be that it is based on kindness and pity for beings that one generates the bodhi resolve.

思惟诸佛复有五事。一者思惟十方过去未来现在诸佛初始发心具烦恼性亦如我今。终成正觉为无上尊。以此缘故发菩提心。二者思惟一切三世诸佛发大勇猛。各各能得无上菩提。若此菩提是可得法我亦应得。缘此事故发菩提心。三者思惟一切三世诸佛发大明慧。于无明[谷-禾+卵][11]中建立胜心积集苦行。皆能自拔超出三界。我亦如是当自拔济。缘此事故发菩提心。四者思惟一切三世诸佛为人中雄。皆度生死烦恼大海。我亦丈夫亦当能度。缘此事故发菩提心。五者思惟一切三世诸佛发大精进。舍身命财求一切智。我今亦当随学诸佛。缘此事故发菩提心。观身过患发菩提心。复有五事。

简体字

思惟諸佛復有五事。一者思惟十方過去未來現在諸佛初始發心具煩惱性亦如我今。終成正覺為無上尊。以此緣故發菩提心。二者思惟一切三世諸佛發大勇猛。各各能得無上菩提。若此菩提是可得法我亦應得。緣此事故發菩提心。三者思惟一切三世諸佛發大明慧。於無明[穀-禾+卵][11]中建立勝心積集苦行。皆能自拔超出三界。我亦如是當自拔濟。緣此事故發菩提心。四者思惟一切三世諸佛為人中雄。皆度生死煩惱大海。我亦丈夫亦當能度。緣此事故發菩提心。五者思惟一切三世諸佛發大精進。捨身命財求一切智。我今亦當隨學諸佛。緣此事故發菩提心。觀身過患發菩提心。復有五事。

正體字

Chapter 2: *Generating the Resolve*

1. CONTEMPLATION OF ALL BUDDHAS

This "contemplation of all buddhas" is itself possessed of five additional circumstantial factors:

First, one may contemplate thus: "When all buddhas of the ten directions of the past, future, and present generated the resolve, they, too, were completely possessed of an afflicted nature in just the very same way that I am now. Still, they finally succeed in realizing the right enlightenment and in becoming those who are unsurpassed in the veneration accorded them." It may be on account of this circumstance that one generates the bodhi resolve.

Second, one may contemplate thus: "All buddhas of the three periods of time bring forth great heroic bravery. Each and every one of them is able to succeed in realizing the unsurpassed bodhi. If this bodhi is in fact a dharma which can be realized, I too ought to realize it myself." It may be on account of this circumstance that one generates the bodhi resolve.

Third, one may contemplate thus: "All buddhas of the three periods of time generate great brilliant wisdom and, even when encased in the shell of ignorance, still establish the supreme resolve, proceed to accumulate the bitter practices, and in every case become able to extricate themselves from the three realms and step entirely beyond them. I, too, should extricate and rescue myself from this situation." It may be on account of this circumstance that one generates the bodhi resolve.

Fourth, one may contemplate thus: "All buddhas of the three periods of time are heroes among men. In every case they have succeeded in crossing beyond the great sea of afflictions arising in the midst of births and deaths. Since I, too, am a real man, I should be able to cross beyond it as well." It may be on account of this circumstance that one generates the bodhi resolve.

Fifth, one may contemplate thus: "All of the buddhas of the three periods of time brought forth the great vigor and relinquished even their physical lives and wealth in the pursuit of all-knowledge. I, too, should follow along in this way, learning from the example of the Buddhas." It may be on account of this circumstance that one generates the bodhi resolve.

2. CONTEMPLATION OF THE BODY'S FAULTS AND PERILOUS ASPECTS

"Contemplation of the faults and perilous aspects of the physical body" is itself possessed of five additional circumstantial factors [conducing to generation of the bodhi resolve]:

简体字	正體字
一者自观我身。五阴四大俱能兴造无量恶业。欲舍离故。二者自观我身。九孔常流臭秽不净。生厌离故。三者自观我身。有贪瞋痴无量烦恼烧然善心。欲除灭故。四者自观我身。如泡如沫念念生灭。是可舍法欲弃捐故。五者自观我身。无明所覆常造恶业。轮迴六趣无利益故。求最胜果发菩提心。复有五事。一者见诸如来。相好庄严光明清彻遇者除恼。为修集故。二者见诸如来。法身常住清净无染。为修集故。三者见诸如来。有戒定慧解脱解脱知见清净法聚。为修集故。	一者自觀我身。五陰四大俱能興造無量惡業。欲捨離故。二者自觀我身。九孔常流臭穢不淨。生厭離故。三者自觀我身。有貪瞋癡無量煩惱燒然善心。欲除滅故。四者自觀我身。如泡如沫念念生滅。是可捨法欲棄捐故。五者自觀我身。無明所覆常造惡業。輪迴六趣無利益故。求最勝果發菩提心。復有五事。一者見諸如來。相好莊嚴光明清徹遇者除惱。為修集故。二者見諸如來。法身常住清淨無染。為修集故。三者見諸如來。有戒定慧解脫解脫知見清淨法聚。為修集故。

First, one may contemplate thus: "My body, consisting as it does of the five aggregates and the four great elements, possesses the ability to commit in flourishing fashion an incalculable number of evil karmic deeds." Hence it may be on account of a desire to abandon this circumstance.

Second, one may contemplate thus: "My body constantly streams forth malodorous filth from nine apertures." Hence it may be on account of having generated renunciation.

Third, one may contemplate thus: "My body is possessed by covetousness, hatred, delusion, and countless afflictions which burn up the wholesome mind." Hence it may be out of a desire to be rid of this circumstance.

Fourth, one may contemplate thus: "My body, [in its fragility], is like a water bubble and like sea foam. It is produced and destroyed in each successive thought-moment and, as such, is worthy of being relinquished." Hence it may be on account of a desire to abandon this circumstance.

Fifth, one may contemplate thus: "My body's [actions] are so blanketed by ignorance that I constantly create evil karmic deeds and continue on with the cycle of rebirths in the six destinies." Hence it may be on account of recognizing that there is no benefit in such a circumstance.

3. Generating Resolve Based on Seeking the Path's Supreme Fruits

"Generating the bodhi resolve based on seeking the most supreme of all fruits [of the Path]" is itself possessed of five additional circumstantial factors:

First, one may observe that the Tathāgatas are adorned with the major marks and subsidiary characteristics and that those who encounter the clear and penetrating quality of their radiance thereby get rid of afflictions. Hence it may be for the sake of cultivating and accumulating [such qualities].

Second, one may observe that the Dharma body of the Tathāgatas abides eternally in a state of purity free of any defilement. Hence it may be for the sake of cultivating and accumulating [just such qualities for oneself].

Third, one may observe that the Tathāgatas possess the pure dharma collections of moral virtue, meditative concentration, wisdom, liberation, and the knowledge and vision associated with liberation. Hence it may be for the sake of cultivating and accumulating [such qualities].

四者见诸如来。有十力四无所畏大悲三念处。为修集故。五者见诸如来。有一切智。怜愍众生慈悲普覆。能为一切愚迷正[12]道。为修集故慈愍众生发菩提心。复有五事。一者见诸众生为无明所缚。二者见诸众生为众苦所缠。三者见诸众生集不善业。四者见诸众生造极重恶。五者见诸众生不修正法。无明所缚复有四事。一者见诸众生为痴爱所惑受大剧苦。二者见诸众生不信因果造作恶业。三者见诸众生舍离正法信受邪道。四者见诸众生。没烦恼河四流所漂。众苦所缠复有四事。一者见诸众生。畏生老病死不求解脱而复造业。

简体字

四者見諸如來。有十力四無所畏大悲三念處。為修集故。五者見諸如來。有一切智。憐愍眾生慈悲普覆。能為一切愚迷正[12]道。為修集故慈愍眾生發菩提心。復有五事。一者見諸眾生為無明所縛。二者見諸眾生為眾苦所纏。三者見諸眾生集不善業。四者見諸眾生造極重惡。五者見諸眾生不修正法。無明所縛復有四事。一者見諸眾生為癡愛所惑受大劇苦。二者見諸眾生不信因果造作惡業。三者見諸眾生捨離正法信受邪道。四者見諸眾生。沒煩惱河四流所漂。眾苦所纏復有四事。一者見諸眾生。畏生老病死不求解脫而復造業。

正體字

Fourth, one may observe that the Tathāgatas possess the ten powers, the four fearlessnesses, the great compassion, and the three stations of mindfulness.[9] Hence it may be for the sake of cultivating and accumulating [such qualities].

Fifth, one may observe that the Tathāgatas possess all-knowledge, that they act out of pity for beings, that their kindness and compassion extend universally to all, and that they are able to serve as guides to the correct path for all who abide in the midst of foolishness and delusion. Hence it may be for the sake of cultivating and accumulating [such qualities].

4. Generating the Bodhi resolve Based on Kindness and Pity

"Generating the bodhi resolve based on kindness and pity for beings" is itself possessed of five additional circumstantial factors:

First, one may observe that beings are tied up by ignorance.

Second, one may observe that beings are bound up by the manifold sorts of suffering.

Third, one may observe that beings are engaged in the accumulation of bad karma.

Fourth, one may observe that beings are engaged in committing the most extremely grave sorts of evil.

Fifth, one may observe that beings fail to cultivate right Dharma.

a. Observing that Beings Are Tied up by Ignorance

"Being tied up by ignorance" is itself possessed of four additional circumstantial factors:

First, one may observe that beings are deceived by delusion and love and consequently undergo extremely intense suffering.

Second, one may observe that beings do not believe in cause and effect and thus commit evil karmic deeds.

Third, one may observe that beings abandon right Dharma while believing in and accepting erroneous paths.

Fourth, one may observe that beings are sunken in the river of afflictions and are swept along by the four currents.[10]

b. Observing that Beings Are Bound up by Manifold Sufferings

"Being bound up by the manifold sorts of sufferings" is itself possessed of four additional circumstantial factors:

First, one may observe that beings fear birth, aging, sickness, and death, but do not seek liberation from them while still continuing to create [negative] karma.

简体字	正體字
二者见诸众生忧悲[p510n01]恼苦而常造作无有休息。三者见诸众生爱别离苦而不觉悟方便染着。四者见诸众生怨憎会苦常起嫌嫉更复造怨。集不善业复有四事。一者见诸众生为爱欲故造作诸恶。二者见诸众生知欲生苦而不舍欲。三者见诸众生虽欲求乐不具戒足。四者见诸众生虽不乐苦造苦不息。造极重恶复有四事。一者见诸众生毁犯重戒虽复忧惧而犹放逸。二者见诸众生兴造极恶五无间业。凶顽自蔽不生惭愧。三者见诸众生谤毁大乘方等正法。专愚自执方起憍慢。四者见诸众生虽怀聪哲而具断	二者見諸眾生憂悲[p510n01]惱苦而常造作無有休息。三者見諸眾生愛別離苦而不覺悟方便染著。四者見諸眾生怨憎會苦常起嫌嫉更復造怨。集不善業復有四事。一者見諸眾生為愛欲故造作諸惡。二者見諸眾生知欲生苦而不捨欲。三者見諸眾生雖欲求樂不具戒足。四者見諸眾生雖不樂苦造苦不息。造極重惡復有四事。一者見諸眾生毀犯重戒雖復憂懼而猶放逸。二者見諸眾生興造極惡五無間業。兇頑自蔽不生慚愧。三者見諸眾生謗毀大乘方等正法。專愚自執方起憍慢。四者見諸眾生雖懷聰哲而具斷

Second, one may observe that beings are beset by worry, lamentation, affliction, and suffering, and yet continue to constantly and ceaselessly create yet more of it.

Third, one may observe that beings endure the suffering of being separated from those they love and yet do not awaken to the means by which they become subject to defiling attachment.

Fourth, one may observe that beings endure the suffering of close proximity to those whom they detest and yet constantly generate hatefulness and thus continue to create yet more adversaries.

 c. Observing that Beings Are Engaged in Accumulating Bad Karma

"Observing that beings are engaged in the accumulation of bad karma" is itself possessed of four additional circumstantial factors:

First, one may observe that beings commit all manner of evil deeds on account of desire.

Second, one may observe that beings realize desire produces suffering and yet still do not forsake desire.

Third, one may observe that, although beings wish to seek out happiness, they still fail to equip themselves with the "feet" of the moral precepts [by which they might proceed thereto].

Fourth, one may observe that, although beings find no pleasure in suffering, they still continue ceaselessly to create suffering.

 d. Observing that Beings Are Engaged in Extremely Grave Evils

"Observing that beings are engaged in committing the most extremely grave sorts of evil" is itself possessed of four additional circumstantial factors:

First, one may observe that beings break the important precepts and, although they thereby become beset by worry and terror, they nonetheless continue to be negligent.

Second, one may observe that beings commit in flourishing fashion the most extreme sorts of evil deeds, including the five karmic deeds entailing non-intermittent retribution. They bury themselves in fierce and inveterate [evil karmic habits] and do not bring forth either a sense of shame or a sense of blame.

Third, one may observe that beings slander the right Dharma of the Great Vehicle's Vaipulya teachings. They devote themselves exclusively to foolish involvement in their own attachments and then generate arrogance based on this.

Fourth, one may observe that, even though beings might cherish intelligence and sagacity, they may nonetheless completely sever

简体字	正體字
善根。反自贡高永无改悔。不修正法复有四事。一者见诸众生生于八难不闻正法不知修善。二者见诸众生值佛出世闻说正法不能受持。三者见诸众生染习外道苦身修业永离出要。四者见诸众生修得非想非非想定谓是涅盘。善报既尽还堕三涂。菩萨见诸众生无明造业长夜受苦。舍离正法迷于出路。为是等故发大慈悲。志求阿耨多罗三藐三菩提。如救头[2]燃。一切众生有苦恼者。我当拔济令无有馀。诸佛子。我今略说初行菩萨缘事发心。若广说者无量无边。	善根。反自貢高永無改悔。不修正法復有四事。一者見諸眾生生於八難不聞正法不知修善。二者見諸眾生值佛出世聞說正法不能受持。三者見諸眾生染習外道苦身修業永離出要。四者見諸眾生修得非想非非想定謂是涅槃。善報既盡還墮三塗。菩薩見諸眾生無明造業長夜受苦。捨離正法迷於出路。為是等故發大慈悲。志求阿耨多羅三藐三菩提。如救頭[2]燃。一切眾生有苦惱者。我當拔濟令無有餘。諸佛子。我今略說初行菩薩緣事發心。若廣說者無量無邊。

their own roots of goodness and, paradoxically, indulge in hypocrisy, never repenting of their errors.

 e. Observing that Beings Fail to Cultivate Right Dharma

"Observing that beings fail to cultivate right Dharma" is itself possessed of four additional circumstantial factors:

First, one may observe that beings are born into the midst of the eight difficulties, do not listen to right Dharma, and do not know to cultivate goodness.

Second, one may observe that beings may encounter the Buddha when he comes into the World, may hear the explanation of right Dharma, and yet still may be unable to accept and uphold it.

Third, one may observe that, in their cultivation of karma, beings engage in the defiled practices of non-Buddhist physical asceticism and then abandon forever the essential means of transcendence.

Fourth, one may observe that beings cultivate and gain the neither perception nor non-perception meditative concentration and then hold the opinion that this constitutes nirvāṇa. Then, once this retribution for goodness comes to an end, they are still compelled to fall once again into the three [wretched] rebirth destinies.

The bodhisattva observes that, through ignorance, beings create [negative] karma and then endure suffering throughout the long night [of time]. They abandon right Dharma and then become confused about what constitutes the road of transcendence. On account of this, one may bring forth the great kindness and the great compassion and resolve to seek *anuttara-samyak-saṃbodhi*, striving then to gain it with the same urgency of action pursued by one striving to save himself when his turban has caught fire.

[He thinks], "Among all beings, those who are beset by bitter afflictions are such as I should extricate and rescue, saving all of them without exception."

 C. Summation on the Causal Bases for Generating the Bodhi resolve

Sons of the Buddha, I have now explained in general terms the conditions serving as bases for generation of the [bodhi] mind on the part of the bodhisattva who has only just taken up the practice [of the Path]. Were one to engage in an extensive explanation of the matter, it would become incalculably vast and boundless in its range.

[*]发菩提心[*]经论。

愿誓品第三。

[0510b03] 菩萨云何发趣菩提。以何业行成就菩提。发心菩萨住乾慧地。先当坚固发于正愿。摄受一切无量众生。我求无上菩提。救护度脱令无有馀。皆令究竟无馀涅盘。是故初始发心大悲为首。以悲心故能发转胜十大正愿。何谓为十。[3]愿我先世及以今身所种善根。以此善根施与一切无边众生。悉共迴向无上菩提。令我此愿念念增长。世世所生常[4]系在心终不忘失。为陀罗尼之所守护。[5]愿我迴向大菩提已。以此善根。于一切生处常得供养一切诸佛。[6]永必不生无佛国土。[7]愿我得生诸佛国已。常得亲近随侍左右如影随形。无

3

The Establishment of Vows

III. CHAPTER 3: THE ESTABLISHMENT OF VOWS
   A. INTRODUCTION TO THE BODHISATTVA'S ESTABLISHMENT OF VOWS

How does the bodhisattva go about setting out towards bodhi? Through which karmic practices does one bring about the complete realization of bodhi? The bodhisattva who has generated the resolve [to gain bodhi] and who abides on "the ground of dry wisdom"[11] should first solidly set forth right vows through which he will draw in all of the incalculably many beings, [proclaiming], "I seek to realize the unsurpassed bodhi and to rescue and liberate everyone without exception so that every one of them is caused to reach all the way to the nirvāṇa without residue."

   B. THE TEN GREAT VOWS

Therefore, in the initial generation of the resolve, it is the great compassion which is foremost. It is on account of the mind of compassion that one becomes able to generate ten ever more superior great right vows. What are those ten? They are:

1. "Regarding those roots of goodness I have planted in previous lives and in this present body, I pray that all of these roots of goodness may be bestowed upon all of the boundlessly many beings and dedicated to the unsurpassed bodhi. May it be that these vows of mine shall grow in each succeeding thought-moment, shall be produced again in each successive lifetime, shall always be bound to my mind, shall never be forgotten, and shall be guarded and retained by *dhāraṇīs*."

2. "Having already dedicated these roots of goodness to bodhi, I pray that on account of these roots of goodness, no matter where I may be reborn, I shall always be able to make offerings to all buddhas and shall definitely never be reborn in a land where there is no buddha."

3. "Having already succeeded in being reborn in the lands of the Buddhas, I pray that I shall always be able to draw personally close to them, shall follow along and serve them in every way (lit. "left-and-right"), shall remain as close to them as a shadow to its form, and shall never become

刹那顷远离诸佛。[8]愿我得亲近佛已。随我所应为我说法。即得成就菩萨五通。[9]愿我成就菩萨五通已。即[10]能通达世谛假名流布。解了第一义谛如真实性。得正法智。[11]愿我得正法智已。以无厌心为众生说。示教利喜皆令开解。[12]愿我能开解诸众生已。以佛神力遍至十方无馀世界。供养诸佛听受正法广摄众生。[13]愿我于诸佛所受正法已。即能随转清净法轮。十方世界一切众生听我法者闻我名者。即得舍离一切烦恼发菩提心。[14]愿我能令一切众生发菩提心已。常随将护除无利益与无量乐。舍身命财摄受众生荷负正法。

简体字

刹那頃遠離諸佛。[8]願我得親近佛已。隨我所應為我說法。即得成就菩薩五通。[9]願我成就菩薩五通已。即[10]能通達世諦假名流布。解了第一義諦如真實性。得正法智。[11]願我得正法智已。以無厭心為眾生說。示教利喜皆令開解。[12]願我能開解諸眾生已。以佛神力遍至十方無餘世界。供養諸佛聽受正法廣攝眾生。[13]願我於諸佛所受正法已。即能隨轉清淨法輪。十方世界一切眾生聽我法者聞我名者。即得捨離一切煩惱發菩提心。[14]願我能令一切眾生發菩提心已。常隨將護除無利益與無量樂。捨身命財攝受眾生荷負正法。

正體字

distantly separated from the Buddhas even for the briefest of moments (lit. *kṣaṇa*)."

4. "Having already succeeded in drawing personally close to the Buddhas, I pray that they will then speak Dharma for my sake in accordance with whatsoever is appropriate for me. May I then straightaway perfect the bodhisattva's five superknowledges."

5. "Having already perfected the bodhisattva's five superknowledges, I pray that I shall thereupon be able to reach a penetrating understanding of worldly truth together with its widespread artificial designations, that I shall also then completely comprehend, in accordance with its genuine nature, the foremost ultimate truth, and that I will gain right-Dharma wisdom."

6. "Having already realized the right-Dharma wisdom, I pray that, free of any thoughts of aversion, I shall then explain it for the sake of beings, instructing them in the teachings, benefiting them, delighting them, and causing them all to develop an understanding of it."

7. "Having already become able to create an understanding [of right Dharma] in beings, I pray that, availing myself of the spiritual power of the Buddhas, I shall be able to go to all worlds without exception everywhere throughout the ten directions, making offerings to the Buddhas, listening to and accepting right Dharma, and extensively drawing in beings [to the Dharma]."

8. "Having already received right Dharma in the abodes of the Buddhas, I pray that I shall thereupon be able to turn the wheel of the pure Dharma in accordance with it. May it then be that all beings of the ten directions' worlds who hear me proclaim the Dharma or who merely hear my name shall then straightaway succeed in abandoning all afflictions and in generating the bodhi resolve."

9. "Having already become able to cause all beings to generate the bodhi resolve, I pray that I may constantly follow along with them, protecting them, ridding them of whatever is unbeneficial, bestowing on them countless sorts of happiness, relinquishing my life and wealth for their sakes, drawing in beings, and taking on the burden of right Dharma."

简体字	正體字
[15]愿我能[16]负荷正法已。虽行正法心无所行。如诸菩萨行于正法。而无所行亦无不行。为化众生不舍正愿。是名发心菩萨十大正愿。此十大愿遍众生界。摄受一切恒沙诸愿。若众[17]生尽我愿乃尽。而众[*]生实不可尽。我此大愿亦无有尽。复次布施是菩提因。摄取一切诸众生故。持戒是菩提因。具足众善满本愿故。忍辱是菩提因。成就三十二相八十随形好故。精进是菩提因。增长善行于诸众生勤教化故。禅定是菩提因。[18]菩萨善自调伏能知众生诸心行故。智慧是菩提因。具足能知诸法性相故。取要言之。六波罗蜜是菩提正因。四无量心三十七品诸万善行共相助成。	[15]願我能[16]負荷正法已。雖行正法心無所行。如諸菩薩行於正法。而無所行亦無不行。為化眾生不捨正願。是名發心菩薩十大正願。此十大願遍眾生界。攝受一切恒沙諸願。若眾[17]生盡我願乃盡。而眾[*]生實不可盡。我此大願亦無有盡。復次布施是菩提因。攝取一切諸眾生故。持戒是菩提因。具足眾善滿本願故。忍辱是菩提因。成就三十二相八十隨形好故。精進是菩提因。增長善行於諸眾生勤教化故。禪定是菩提因。[18]菩薩善自調伏能知眾生諸心行故。智慧是菩提因。具足能知諸法性相故。取要言之。六波羅蜜是菩提正因。四無量心三十七品諸萬善行共相助成。

10. "Having already become able to take on the burden of right Dharma, I pray that, even though I shall then practice in accordance with right Dharma, my mind shall nonetheless have nothing whatsoever which it practices. May it be that, in this, I shall conform with the way that the bodhisattvas themselves practice right Dharma and yet have nothing whatsoever which they either practice or do not practice."

For the sake of carrying on the transformative teaching of beings, one never relinquishes right vows. This is what is meant by the ten great right vows of the bodhisattva who has brought forth the resolve [to realize unsurpassed bodhi].

These ten great vows extend everywhere to all realms of beings and subsume all vows as numerous as the Ganges' sands. [Hence one reflects thus:] "If beings were to come to an end, then and only then would my vows then come to an end. However, beings are truly endless. Therefore these great vows of mine shall also never come to an end."

C. THE SIX *PĀRAMITĀS* AND RELATED PRACTICES AS CAUSES OF BODHI

Additionally, giving serves as a cause of bodhi because it draws in all beings.

Upholding the moral precepts is a cause of bodhi because it leads to the perfection of the many sorts of goodness and brings about the fulfillment of one's original vows.

Patience serves as a cause of bodhi because it brings about the perfection of the thirty-two major marks and eighty subsidiary characteristics.

Vigor is a cause of bodhi because it brings about the growth of the practice of goodness and brings about the diligent teaching and transforming of all beings.

Dhyāna absorption is a cause of bodhi because, resorting to it, the bodhisattva skillfully trains and disciplines himself while also becoming able to perceive all of the mental actions of beings.

Wisdom is a cause of bodhi because, resorting to it, one becomes able to perfectly know the nature and characteristics of all of the dharmas.

To sum up the essentials, the six *pāramitās* constitute the correct causes for the realization of bodhi. The four immeasurable minds, the thirty-seven wings of enlightenment, and all of the myriad good practices all work cooperatively together in assisting its perfect realization.

若菩萨修集六波罗蜜。随其所行。渐渐得近阿耨多罗三藐三菩提。诸佛子。求菩提者[19]应不放逸。放逸之行能坏善根。若菩萨制伏六根不放逸者。是人能修六波罗蜜。菩萨发心先建至诚立决定誓。立誓之人终不放逸懈怠慢缓。何以故。立决定誓。有五事持故。一者能坚固其心。二者能制伏烦恼。三者能遮放逸。四者能破五盖。五者能勤修行六波罗蜜。如佛所赞。

如来大智尊。显说功德证。忍慧福业力。誓愿力最胜。

[0510c22] 云何立誓。若有人来种种求索。我于尔时随有施与。乃至不生一念悭悋之心。若生恶心如弹指顷。以施因缘求净报者。我即[20]欺十方世界无量无边阿僧只现在诸

简体字

若菩薩修集六波羅蜜。隨其所行。漸漸得近阿耨多羅三藐三菩提。諸佛子。求菩提者[19]應不放逸。放逸之行能壞善根。若菩薩制伏六根不放逸者。是人能修六波羅蜜。菩薩發心先建至誠立決定誓。立誓之人終不放逸懈怠慢緩。何以故。立決定誓。有五事持故。一者能堅固其心。二者能制伏煩惱。三者能遮放逸。四者能破五蓋。五者能勤修行六波羅蜜。如佛所讚。

如來大智尊。顯說功德證。忍慧福業力。誓願力最勝。

[0510c22] 云何立誓。若有人來種種求索。我於爾時隨有施與。乃至不生一念慳悋之心。若生惡心如彈指頃。以施因緣求淨報者。我即[20]欺十方世界無量無邊阿僧祇現在諸

正體字

If the bodhisattva cultivates and accumulates [skill in the practice of] the six *pāramitās*, as befits the practices he has taken up, he gradually succeeds in drawing near to *anuttara-samyak-saṃbodhi*.

D. The Importance of Refraining from Negligence

Sons of the Buddha, whosoever seeks to realize bodhi should refrain from negligence. Negligent practice is able to destroy one's roots of goodness. If a bodhisattva controls and disciplines the six sense faculties and remains free of negligence in this, such a person will be able to cultivate the six *pāramitās*.

E. Making Definitely-Resolved Vows as Supporting Five Endeavors

When the bodhisattva generates the resolve, he first establishes definite vows set forth with ultimate sincerity. A person who establishes such vows never allows himself to become negligent, indolent, or relaxed in his practice. Why not? This is because the establishment of definite vows supports five types of actions:

First, it is able to make one's resolve solid. Second, it is able to control and subdue the afflictions. Third, it is able to deflect one from falling into negligence. Fourth, it is able to destroy the five hindrances. And fifth, it is able to bring about the diligent cultivation of the six *pāramitās*.

F. The Buddha's Own Praise of the Unsurpassed Power of Vows

This accords with the Buddha's own praise [of vows]:

The Tathāgata, the greatly wise Bhagavān,
Proclaimed what brings about realization of meritorious qualities:
In the power held by patience, wisdom, or meritorious karma,
It is the power of vows which is most superior [in its influence].

G. Establishing Six Resolutions in Support of the Six Perfections

In what manner does one go about establishing vows? [One invokes one's resolve as follows, thinking]:

"In instances where some person comes making all sorts of demands, I shall then give to him whatever I possess, even to the point that I will refrain from generating a single thought influenced by miserliness.

"Were I to generate an evil thought in reaction to this circumstance even for the momentary duration of a finger snap and yet still seek a pure karmic reward from the causes and conditions associated with such giving, I would then straightaway be cheating all of the countless and boundlessly many *asaṃkhyeyas* of present-

佛。于未来世亦当必定不成阿耨多罗三藐三菩提。若我持戒。乃至失命。建立净心誓无改悔。若我修忍。为他侵害乃至割截。常生慈爱誓无恚碍。若我修精进。遭逢寒暑王贼水火师子虎狼无水谷处。要必坚强其心誓不退没。若我修禅。为外事所娆不得摄心。[p511n01]要系念在境。誓不暂起非法乱想。若我修集智慧。观一切法如实性。随顺受持。于善不善有为无为生死涅盘。不起二见。若我心悔恚碍退没乱想。起于二见如弹指顷而。以戒忍精进禅智求净报者。我即[*]欺十方世界无量无边阿僧只现在诸佛。于未来世。亦当必定不成阿耨多罗三藐三菩提。菩萨以十大愿持正法行。以六大誓制

简体字

佛。於未來世亦當必定不成阿耨多羅三藐三菩提。若我持戒。乃至失命。建立淨心誓無改悔。若我修忍。為他侵害乃至割截。常生慈愛誓無恚礙。若我修精進。遭逢寒暑王賊水火師子虎狼無水穀處。要必堅強其心誓不退沒。若我修禪。為外事所嬈不得攝心。[p511n01]要繫念在境。誓不暫起非法亂想。若我修集智慧。觀一切法如實性。隨順受持。於善不善有為無為生死涅槃。不起二見。若我心悔恚礙退沒亂想。起於二見如彈指頃而。以戒忍精進禪智求淨報者。我即[*]欺十方世界無量無邊阿僧祇現在諸佛。於未來世。亦當必定不成阿耨多羅三藐三菩提。菩薩以十大願持正法行。以六大誓制

正體字

era buddhas throughout the worlds of the ten directions and would thereby be ensuring that I shall definitely not be able to realize *anuttara-samyak-saṃbodhi* in the future.

"In upholding the moral precepts, I establish pure-minded vows to remain free of deviation or regret, even where adherence to the precepts might cause me to lose my life.

"In instances where I may be cultivating patience, even where I might be attacked, injured, or even sliced apart, I shall constantly generate lovingly-kind vows free of any sort of interference by hatefulness.

"In instances where I cultivate vigor, even where I might encounter circumstances involving cold, heat, royal minions, bandits, floods, fires, lions, tigers, wolves, drought, or famine, I must nonetheless solidify and strengthen my resolve so that there is no retreat or sinking away of vows.

"In instances where I cultivate dhyāna absorption, even where I am disturbed by external circumstances threatening to make it impossible to focus the mind, it is essential to bind the mind to the objective sphere, vowing to refrain from bringing forth even briefly any sort of distracted thought which is contrary to Dharma.

"In instances where I cultivate the accumulation of wisdom, I contemplate all dharmas in accordance with their true nature, continuing to adaptively uphold and maintain this contemplation even in the midst of that which is good, that which is not good, that which is conditioned, that which is unconditioned, that which is in the sphere of births and deaths, and that which is identical to nirvāṇa, never bringing forth any duality based views in any of those circumstances.

"In instances where my mind might fall prey to the hindrances of regret or anger, were I to retreat and sink into such distracted thought that, even for the duration of a finger snap, I brought forth duality-based views through which I might [instead] seek pure karmic rewards arising from moral virtue, patience, vigor, dhyāna meditation, or wisdom, I would thereby cheat all of the countless and boundlessly many *asaṃkhyeyas* of present-era buddhas throughout the ten-directions' worlds and would thereby definitely fail to realize *anuttara-samyak-saṃbodhi* in the future."

H. The Importance of the Ten Vows and Six Resolutions to Bodhi

The bodhisattva employs the ten great vows to maintain his practice of right Dharma and resorts to the six great pledges to control

放逸心。必能精勤修集六波罗蜜。成阿耨多罗三藐三菩提。	放逸心。必能精勤修集六波羅蜜。成阿耨多羅三藐三菩提。
简体字	正體字

the mind's tendency to drift into negligence. In doing so, he will definitely be able to diligently cultivate the six *pāramitās* and will definitely succeed in realizing *anuttara-samyak-saṃbodhi*.

[*]发菩提心[*]经论。

[2]檀波罗蜜品第四。

[0511a13] 云何菩萨修行布施布施若为自利[3]他利及二俱利。如是布施。则能庄严菩提之道。菩萨为欲调伏众生令离苦恼。是故行施。修行施者于己财物常生舍心于来求者。起尊重心如。父母师长善知识想。于贫穷下贱起怜愍心如一子想。随所须与心喜恭敬。是名菩萨初修施心。修布施故善名流布。随所生处财宝丰盈。是名自利。能[4]令众生心得满足。教化调伏使无悭悋。是名利他。以己所修无相大施。化诸众生令同己利。是名俱利。

简体字

[*]發菩提心[*]經論。

[2]檀波羅蜜品第四。

[0511a13] 云何菩薩修行布施布施若為自利[3]他利及二俱利。如是布施。則能莊嚴菩提之道。菩薩為欲調伏眾生令離苦惱。是故行施。修行施者於己財物常生捨心於來求者。起尊重心如。父母師長善知識想。於貧窮下賤起憐愍心如一子想。隨所須與心喜恭敬。是名菩薩初修施心。修布施故善名流布。隨所生處財寶豐盈。是名自利。能[4]令眾生心得滿足。教化調伏使無慳悋。是名利他。以己所修無相大施。化諸眾生令同己利。是名俱利。

正體字

4
Dāna Pāramitā

IV. CHAPTER 4: THE PERFECTION OF GIVING
   A. THREE KINDS OF BENEFIT AND PATH ADORNMENT ARISING FROM GIVING

How does the bodhisattva go about cultivating giving? If giving is cultivated for the sake of bringing about self-benefit, benefit of others, and the combined benefit of both, one becomes able thereby to adorn the path to bodhi.

   1. RIGHT MOTIVATION IN THE PRACTICE OF GIVING

In his cultivation of giving, the bodhisattva is motivated by a wish to so train and discipline beings that they are caused to abandon suffering and affliction.

One who cultivates the practice of giving constantly brings forth the motivation to relinquish his own material wealth to whosoever might come and seek to obtain it. In doing so, he brings forth a mind of veneration and esteem comparable to the thoughts he would bring forth in relation to his father, mother, teachers, elders, or good spiritual guide.

Even towards those who are poverty-stricken and of the most lowly social station, he brings forth thoughts of pity comparable to those he would have towards his only son. He gives whatever is needed with a delighted and respectful mind. This is what qualifies as the mind of giving as initially cultivated by the bodhisattva.

   2. SELF-BENEFIT

On account of cultivating the practice of giving, one's fine reputation spreads all about and, no matter where one is reborn, one's wealth and jewels become luxuriously abundant. This is what is meant by "self-benefit."

   3. BENEFIT OF OTHERS

Where one is able to cause the minds of beings to become satisfied, where one is able to transform them through teaching, and where one is able to train and discipline them in a way whereby they are caused to become free of miserliness, this is what is meant by "benefit of others."

   4. COMBINED BENEFIT

On the basis of that signless great giving[12] which one has cultivated, one teaches beings, thus causing them to gain benefit identical to one's own. This is what is meant by "combined benefit."

因修布施获得转轮王位。摄受一切无量众生。乃至得佛无尽法藏。是名庄严菩提之道。施有三种。一以法施。二无畏施。三财物施。以法施者。劝人受戒修出家心。为坏邪见说断常四倒众恶过患。分别开示真谛之义。赞精进功德。说放逸过恶。是名法施。若有众生怖畏王者师子虎狼水火盗贼。菩萨见已能为救护。名无畏施。自于财物施而不悋。上至珍宝象马车乘缯帛谷麦衣服饮食。下至麨[5]搏一缕之[6]綎若多若少称求者意随所须与。是名财施。财施[7]复有五种。一者至心施。二者信心施。三者随时施。四者自手施。五者如法施。

因修布施獲得轉輪王位。攝受一切無量眾生。乃至得佛無盡法藏。是名莊嚴菩提之道。施有三種。一以法施。二無畏施。三財物施。以法施者。勸人受戒修出家心。為壞邪見說斷常四倒眾惡過患。分別開示真諦之義。讚精進功德。說放逸過惡。是名法施。若有眾生怖畏王者師子虎狼水火盜賊。菩薩見已能為救護。名無畏施。自於財物施而不悋。上至珍寶象馬車乘繒帛穀麥衣服飲食。下至麨[5]搏一縷之[6]綎若多若少稱求者意隨所須與。是名財施。財施[7]復有五種。一者至心施。二者信心施。三者隨時施。四者自手施。五者如法施。

简体字　　　　　　　　　正體字

5. ADORNING THE PATH OF BODHI THROUGH GIVING

On account of cultivating giving, one gains the throne of the wheel-turning king, draws in all of the incalculably many beings, and becomes able even to gain the inexhaustible Dharma treasury of the Buddha. This is what is meant by "adorning the path to bodhi."

B. THE THREE TYPES OF GIVING

Giving is of three types. The first is Dharma giving. The second is the giving of fearlessness. The third is giving of material wealth.

1. THE GIVING OF DHARMA

As for the giving of Dharma, one encourages people to take on the precepts and to cultivate the mind of those who have left the home life. For the sake of destroying erroneous views, one explains the faults and perils inherent in the manifold evils flowing from annihilationism, eternalism, and the four inverted views. One distinguishes and explains the meaning of ultimate truth. One praises the meritorious qualities of vigor, explaining the faults and evils inherent in negligence. This is what is meant by the giving of Dharma.

2. THE GIVING OF FEARLESSNESS

In an instance where the bodhisattva observes beings beset by fear of representatives of the King, lions, tigers, wolves, floods, fire, bandits, or insurgents, he is able then to rescue and protect them. This is what is meant by the giving of fearlessness.

3. THE DEFINITION AND SCOPE OF THE GIVING OF MATERIAL WEALTH

Where one gives material wealth and remains free of miserliness, even where such giving extends up to jewels, elephants, horses, carriages, silks, grains, clothing, food and drink, and even where such giving extends down to a scoop of fried flour or a strand of thread—and where one matches the aims of the supplicants by bestowing on them whatsoever they may need, no matter whether it be much or whether it be little—this is what is meant by the giving of material wealth.

1) FIVE SUBCATEGORIES OF THE GIVING OF MATERIAL WEALTH

The giving of material wealth is itself possessed of five additional categories:
First, giving done with an ultimately sincere mind;
Second, giving done based on faith;
Third, giving which is appropriate to the time;
Fourth, giving which is done with one's very own hands;
Fifth, giving which accords with Dharma.

简体字	正體字
所不应施复有五事。非理求财不以施人。物不净故酒及毒药不以施人。乱众生故。[8]置罗机网不以施人。恼众生故。刀[9]杖弓箭不以施人。害众生故。音乐女色不以施人。坏净心故。取要言之。不如法物恼乱众生。不以施人。自馀一切能令众生得安乐者。名如法施。乐施之人。复获五种名闻善利。一者常得亲近一切贤圣。二者一切众生之所乐见。三者入大众时人所宗敬。四者好名善誉流闻十方。五者能为菩提作上妙因。菩萨之人名一切施。一切施者非谓多财。谓施心也。	所不應施復有五事。非理求財不以施人。物不淨故酒及毒藥不以施人。亂眾生故。[8]置羅機網不以施人。惱眾生故。刀[9]杖弓箭不以施人。害眾生故。音樂女色不以施人。壞淨心故。取要言之。不如法物惱亂眾生。不以施人。自餘一切能令眾生得安樂者。名如法施。樂施之人。復獲五種名聞善利。一者常得親近一切賢聖。二者一切眾生之所樂見。三者入大眾時人所宗敬。四者好名善譽流聞十方。五者能為菩提作上妙因。菩薩之人名一切施。一切施者非謂多財。謂施心也。

Chapter 4: *The Perfection of Giving*

2) Five Categories of Wrong Giving

That which should not be given is itself also possessed of five additional categories:

1. Items of material wealth obtained in an unprincipled manner should not be given to people because such items do not qualify as pure [gifts].
2. Intoxicants and toxic herbs are such as one does not give to people because they instill confusion in other beings.
3. Snares, traps, and animal nets are such as one does not give to people because they torment beings.
4. Swords, cudgels, bows, and arrows are such as one does not give to people because they injure beings.
5. Music and sensual encounters with women are such as one does not give to people because they bring about destruction of the pure mind.

3) Summary of Wrong and Right Giving

To sum up the essentials, whatever does not accord with Dharma or whatever torments or confuses beings should not be given to people. Whatever else one possesses which may cause beings to experience happiness qualifies as gifts which accord with Dharma.

C. Five Additional Benefits of Delighting in Giving

People who delight in giving gain five additional kinds of renown and wholesome benefit:

First, they always succeed in drawing personally close to all of the Bhadras and the Āryas.

Second, they become such as all beings are happy to see.

Third, when they enter the Great Assembly, they are revered by others.

Fourth, their fine name and good reputation flow everywhere and become renowned throughout the ten directions.

Fifth, they are thereby able to create superior and marvelous causes for the realization of bodhi.

D. Universality in Giving, the Defining Characteristic of a Bodhisattva

One who is a bodhisattva is defined by being one who is universal in his giving. Being one who is universal in his giving does not refer to a circumstance involving an abundance of material wealth but rather refers instead to possessing a mind inclined toward giving.

简体字	正體字
如法求财持以布施。名一切施。以清净心无谄曲施。名一切施。见贫穷者怜愍心施。名一切施。见厄苦者慈悲心施。名一切施。居贫少财而能用施。名一切施。爱重宝物开意能施。名一切施。不观持戒毁戒田非田施。名一切施。不求人天妙善乐施。名一切施。志求无上大菩提施。名一切施。欲施施[10]时施已不悔。名一切施。若以华施。[11]具陀罗尼七觉华故。若以香施。具戒定慧熏涂身故若以果施。具足成就无漏果故。	如法求財持以布施。名一切施。以清淨心無諂曲施。名一切施。見貧窮者憐愍心施。名一切施。見厄苦者慈悲心施。名一切施。居貧少財而能用施。名一切施。愛重寶物開意能施。名一切施。不觀持戒毀戒田非田施。名一切施。不求人天妙善樂施。名一切施。志求無上大菩提施。名一切施。欲施施[10]時施已不悔。名一切施。若以華施。[11]具陀羅尼七覺華故。若以香施。具戒定慧熏塗身故若以果施。具足成就無漏果故。

Where one takes up material wealth sought out in accordance with Dharma and uses it in giving, this accords with universality in giving.

Where one uses a pure mind free of deception in one's giving, this accords with universality in giving.

Where one observes those who are poverty-stricken and, with a mind inclined towards pity, proceeds to give to them, this accords with universality in giving.

Where one observes those who are ensconced in hardship and suffering and, with a mind of kindness and compassion, proceeds to give to them, this accords with universality in giving.

Where one abides in poverty and possesses but little material wealth, yet one is nonetheless able to give something useful, this accords with universality in giving.

Where one loves and esteems precious things, but then is able to free up his mind and give them as gifts, this accords with universality in giving.

Where one disregards whether the recipient is one who upholds the precepts or breaks the precepts and also disregards whether the recipient constitutes a field of blessings or does not qualify as a field of blessings, this accords with universality in giving.

Where one does not give out of a desire to acquire the marvelously fine bliss available in human or celestial rebirths, this accords with universality in giving.

Where one gives in the course of seeking to realize the unsurpassed bodhi, this accords with universality in giving.

Where one experiences no regrets when one is about to give, when one is actually giving, and also after one has given, this accords with universality in giving.

E. Types of Giving as Bases for Corresponding Karmic Fruits

In a case where one gives flowers, it contributes to the causal bases for obtaining the flowers of the *dhāraṇīs* and the seven limbs of bodhi.

In a case where one gives incenses, it contributes to the causal bases for [the incense-like fragrances of] moral virtue, meditative concentration, and wisdom imbuing and applying themselves to one's own person.

In a case where one gives fruit, it contributes to the causal bases for perfecting the fruits [of the Path] which are free of outflow impurities.

若以食施。具足命辯色力乐故。以衣服施。具清净色除无惭愧故。以灯明施。具足佛眼照了一切诸法性故以象马车乘施。得无上乘具足神通故以缨络施。具足八十随形好故。以珍宝施。具足大人三十二相故。以筋力仆使施。具佛十力四无畏故。取要言之。乃至国城妻子头目手足。举身施与心无恪惜。为得无上菩提度众生故。菩萨摩诃萨修行布施。不见财物施者受者。以无相故。是则具足[12]檀波罗蜜。

简体字

若以食施。具足命辯色力樂故。以衣服施。具清淨色除無慚愧故。以燈明施。具足佛眼照了一切諸法性故以象馬車乘施。得無上乘具足神通故以纓絡施。具足八十隨形好故。以珍寶施。具足大人三十二相故。以筋力僕使施。具佛十力四無畏故。取要言之。乃至國城妻子頭目手足。舉身施與心無恪惜。為得無上菩提度眾生故。菩薩摩訶薩修行布施。不見財物施者受者。以無相故。是則具足[12]檀波羅蜜。

正體字

In a case where one gives food, it contributes to the causal bases for possessing long life, eloquence, fine appearance, physical strength, and happiness.

In a case where one gives clothing, it contributes to the causal bases for gaining a pure physical form and for ridding oneself of any absence of a sense of shame or sense of blame.

In a case where one gives the light of lamps, it contributes to the causal bases for gaining the buddha eye's complete illumination of the nature of all dharmas.

In a case where one gives conveyances drawn by elephants or horses, it contributes to the causal bases for gaining the unsurpassed vehicle and for perfecting the spiritual superknowledges.

In a case where one gives [prayer-bead] necklaces, this giving contributes to the causal bases for gaining the eighty subsidiary characteristics.

In a case where one gives precious jewels, it contributes to the causal basis for gaining the thirty-two major marks of a great man.

In a case where one gives muscle power or provides servants, it contributes to the causal bases for gaining the ten powers and four fearlessnesses of a buddha.

F. Summation on the Bodhisattva's Cultivation of Giving

To sum up the essentials, one may even go so far as to give up one's country, city, wife, sons, head, eyes, hands, feet, or entire body, giving them with a mind free of miserliness or self-cherishing, all for the sake of realizing the unsurpassed bodhi and bringing beings across to liberation.

G. The Essence of the Bodhisattva's Perfection of Giving

When the bodhisattva, *mahāsattva* cultivates giving, he does not perceive the existence of any material wealth, of any benefactor, or of any recipient. This is because they are devoid of any [inherently-existent] characteristic signs. If one cultivates in this manner, he will then succeed in perfecting *dāna pāramitā*.

[*]发菩提心[*]经论。

尸罗波罗蜜品第五。

[0511c08] 云何菩萨修行持戒。持戒若为自利他利及二俱利。如是持戒。则能庄严菩提之道。菩萨为欲调伏众生令离苦恼。是故持戒。修持戒者。悉净一切身口意业。于不善行心能舍远。善能呵嘖恶行毁禁。于小罪中心常恐怖。是名菩萨初持戒心。修持戒故。远离一切诸恶过患。常生善处。是名自利。教化众生令不犯恶。是名利他。以己所修向菩提戒。化诸众生令同己利。是名俱利。因修持戒。获得离欲乃至

5
Śīla Pāramitā

V. Chapter 5: The Perfection of Moral Virtue
  A. Three Kinds of Benefit and Path Adornment from Moral Virtue

How does the bodhisattva go about cultivating the observance of the moral precepts? If one cultivates the moral precepts for the sake of bringing about self-benefit, benefit of others, and the combined benefit of both, one thus becomes able to adorn the path to bodhi.

    1. Right Motivation in the Practice of Moral Virtue

In his cultivation of the moral precepts, the bodhisattva is motivated by a wish to so train and discipline beings that they are caused to abandon suffering and affliction.

One who cultivates the observance of the moral precepts entirely purifies all karmic deeds of body, mouth, and mind. He becomes able to relinquish and leave far behind any thoughts inclined toward unwholesome actions. He becomes well able to rebuke himself for any tendency toward evil actions or toward transgressing the moral prohibitions. His mind remains constantly fearful of committing even minor karmic offenses.

This is what qualifies as the mind observant of moral virtue as initially cultivated by the bodhisattva.

    2. Self Benefit

Through cultivating observance of moral precepts, one leaves behind all faults and calamities linked to evil deeds and is always reborn in a good place. This is what is meant by "self-benefit."

    3. Benefit of Others

One transforms beings through teaching and thus causes them to refrain from committing evil deeds. This is what is meant by "benefit of others."

    4. Combined Benefit

Through the moral precepts conducive to bodhi which one has personally cultivated, one teaches beings and thereby causes them to gain benefit identical to one's own. This is what is meant by "combined benefit."

    5. Adorning the Path of Bodhi through Moral Virtue

On account of cultivating the observance of the moral precepts, one achieves success in abandoning desire and so forth on up to success

[13]漏尽成最正觉。是名庄严菩提之道。戒有三种。一者身。二者口。三者心。持身戒者。永离一切杀盗婬行。不夺物命不侵他财不犯外色。又亦不为杀等因缘及其方便。不以杖木瓦石伤害众生。若物属他他所受用。一草一叶不与不取。又亦未尝眄睐细色。于四威仪恭谨详审。是名身戒。持口戒者。断除一切妄语两舌恶口绮语。常不欺诳离间和合。诽谤毁訾文饰言辞。及造方便恼触于人。言则至诚柔软忠信。言常饶益劝化修善。是名口戒。

简体字

[13]漏盡成最正覺。是名莊嚴菩提之道。戒有三種。一者身。二者口。三者心。持身戒者。永離一切殺盜婬行。不奪物命不侵他財不犯外色。又亦不為殺等因緣及其方便。不以杖木瓦石傷害眾生。若物屬他他所受用。一草一葉不與不取。又亦未嘗眄睞細色。於四威儀恭謹詳審。是名身戒。持口戒者。斷除一切妄語兩舌惡口綺語。常不欺誑離間和合。誹謗毀訾文飾言辭。及造方便惱觸於人。言則至誠柔軟忠信。言常饒益勸化修善。是名口戒。

正體字

in ending the outflow impurities and success in realization of the most right of all enlightenments. This is what is meant by "adorning the path to bodhi."

B. The Three Types of Moral Precepts

Moral precepts are of three types. The first consists of those prohibitions which relate to the body. The second consists of those which relate to the mouth. The third consists of those which relate to the mind.

1. The Moral precepts Associated with the Body

As for observing the moral precepts associated with the body, one eternally abandons all killing, stealing, and sexual conduct.[13] One refrains from stealing away the lives of beings, refrains from intruding upon the wealth of others, and refrains from transgressing in the sphere of outward physical forms.

Additionally, one refrains from involvement in any of the causes, conditions, or means associated with killing or any of the other transgressions. One does not injure beings with staves, tiles, or stones. In an instance where some object belongs to someone else or is being used by someone else, so long as it has not been given, one does not take it, even if it be something so minor as a blade of grass or a leaf.

Additionally, one never so much as casts a sidelong glance at even the most minor displays of physical forms. In the four types of stately comportment one remains respectful, careful, and closely observant [of the correct standards]. This is what is meant by the moral precepts associated with the body.

2. The Moral precepts Associated with the Mouth

As for observing the moral precepts associated with the mouth, one cuts off and eliminates all false speech, divisive speech, harsh speech, and frivolous speech. One never deceives others, causes estrangement among those who are united, engages in slander, ruins another's reputation, or artificially adorns one's words and speech. Nor does one create the means through which another person may become afflicted by torment.

When one speaks, his discourse is imbued with utmost sincerity, gentleness, loyalty, and trustworthiness. One's words are always beneficial, encouraging, and conducive to transformative teaching and the cultivation of goodness. This is what is meant by the moral precepts associated with the mouth.

简体字	正體字
持心戒者。除灭贪欲瞋恚邪见。常修软心不作过罪。信是罪业得恶果报。思惟力故不造诸恶。于轻罪中生极重想。设误作者恐怖忧悔。于众生所不起瞋恼。见众生已生爱念心。知恩报恩心无悭恪。乐作福德常以化人。常修慈心怜愍一切。是名心戒。是十善业戒。有五事利益。一者能制恶行。二者能作善心。三者能遮烦恼。四者成就净心。五者能增长戒。若人善修不放逸行。具足正念分别善恶。当知是人决定能修十善业戒。八万四千无量戒品。悉皆摄在十善戒中。是	持心戒者。除滅貪欲瞋恚邪見。常修軟心不作過罪。信是罪業得惡果報。思惟力故不造諸惡。於輕罪中生極重想。設誤作者恐怖憂悔。於眾生所不起瞋惱。見眾生已生愛念心。知恩報恩心無慳恪。樂作福德常以化人。常修慈心憐愍一切。是名心戒。是十善業戒。有五事利益。一者能制惡行。二者能作善心。三者能遮煩惱。四者成就淨心。五者能增長戒。若人善修不放逸行。具足正念分別善惡。當知是人決定能修十善業戒。八萬四千無量戒品。悉皆攝在十善戒中。是

3. The Moral Precepts Associated with the Mind

As for observing the moral precepts associated with the mind, one eliminates desire, hatred, and wrong views, constantly cultivates a pliant mind, and refrains from committing karmic transgressions. One believes that this particular karmic offense will result in that particular bad resulting karmic retribution. By resorting to the power of meditative contemplation, one refrains from committing any sort of evil act.

Even with respect to minor karmic offenses, one generates thoughts by which one regards them as extremely serious. In the event that one errs and commits such an offense, then he becomes filled with fearfulness, worry, and regret.

With respect to other beings, one refrains from bringing forth any hatefulness or torment towards them. Whenever one observes other beings, he brings forth thoughts of fond mindfulness towards them. One recognizes the kindnesses of others, repays kindnesses, and maintains a mind free of miserliness. One delights in doing meritorious deeds and constantly uses them as means to teach others. One constantly cultivates the mind of kindness and extends pity to all. This is what is meant by the moral precepts associated with the mind.

4. Five Benefits Arising from the Precepts of the Ten Good Karmas

These moral precepts implicit in the ten good karmic deeds bring about five sorts of beneficial circumstances:

First, one becomes able to control evil actions.

Second, one becomes able to create a wholesome mind.

Third, one becomes able to block off the arising of afflictions.

Fourth, one perfects a pure mind.

Fifth, one becomes able to bring about growth in one's practice of the moral precepts.

5. Summary Discussion of the Precepts of the Ten Good Karmas

In a case where a person skillfully cultivates non-negligent practice and perfects the right mindfulness which distinguishes between good and evil, one should realize that this person is definitely able to cultivate the moral precepts contained within the ten good karmic deeds.

The countless aspects involved in the eighty-four thousand categories of moral precepts are all contained within the moral precepts contained within the ten good karmic deeds. These moral

十善戒能为一切善戒根本。断身口意恶。能制一切不善之法。故名为戒。戒有五种。一者波罗提木叉戒。二者定共戒。三者无漏戒。四者摄根戒。五者无作戒。白四羯磨从师而受。名波罗提木叉戒。根本四禅四未到禅。是名定共戒。根本四禅初禅未到。名无漏戒[p512n01]收摄诸根修正念心。见闻觉知色声香味触不生放逸。名摄根戒。舍身后世更不作恶。名无作戒。菩萨修戒不与声闻辟支佛共。以不共故名善持戒。善

十善戒能為一切善戒根本。斷身口意惡。能制一切不善之法。故名為戒。戒有五種。一者波羅提木叉戒。二者定共戒。三者無漏戒。四者攝根戒。五者無作戒。白四羯磨從師而受。名波羅提木叉戒。根本四禪四未到禪。是名定共戒。根本四禪初禪未到。名無漏戒[p512n01]收攝諸根修正念心。見聞覺知色聲香味觸不生放逸。名攝根戒。捨身後世更不作惡。名無作戒。菩薩修戒不與聲聞辟支佛共。以不共故名善持戒。善

简体字　　　　　　　　　　正體字

precepts included in the ten good karmic deeds are able to serve as the root of all precepts associated with goodness. It is through the cutting off of all evils associated with the body, mouth, and mind that one becomes able to control all unwholesome dharmas. It is on this basis that one defines moral precepts as such.

C. THE FIVE CATEGORIES OF MORAL PRECEPTS

There are five categories of moral precepts:

First, the *pratimokṣa* moral precepts;
Second, the moral precepts linked to meditative concentration;
Third, the moral precepts associated with the absence of out-flow impurities;
Fourth, moral precepts involving withdrawing sense faculties;
Fifth, spontaneous moral precepts involving no intentional effort.

Those precepts taken on in the context of the four proclamations occurring during [official Sangha] *karman* proceedings are referred to as the *pratimokṣa* moral precepts.

Moral precept observance associated with acquisition of the four basic dhyānas and the four dhyāna preliminary stations constitutes what is referred to as the moral precepts linked to meditative concentration.

Moral precept observance associated with the four basic dhyānas and the preliminary station at the threshold of the first dhyāna may qualify as circumstances involving precept observance free of out-flow impurities.

When one draws in the sense faculties and cultivates a mind characterized by right mindfulness which, in its seeing, hearing, awareness, and knowing permits of no negligence regarding forms, sounds, smells, tastes, or touchables, this is what constitutes moral precept observance involving withdrawing the sense faculties.

When, having already relinquished this body, one continues to refrain from committing evil deeds even after rebirth into a subsequent existence, this is what is referred to as spontaneous moral precepts involving no intentional effort.

D. RATIONALES FOR OBSERVING PRECEPTS LINKED TO SPECIFIC PATH PRACTICES

A bodhisattva's cultivation of the moral precepts is of a class not held in common with either the Śrāvaka Disciples or the Pratyekabuddhas. It is because it is of a sort "not held in common," that it qualifies as "skillfully upholding the moral precepts." On account of skillfully

简体字	正體字
持戒故则能利益一切众生。持慈心戒。救护众生令安乐故。持悲心戒。忍受诸苦拔[2]危难故。持喜心戒。[3]欢乐修善不懈怠故。持舍心戒。怨亲平等离爱恚故。持惠施戒。教化调伏诸众生故持忍辱戒。心常柔软无恚[*]碍故。持精进戒。善业日增不退还故。持禅定戒。离欲不善长禅[4]支故。持智慧戒。多闻善根无厌足故。持亲近善知识戒。助成菩提无上道故。持[5]远离恶知识戒。舍离三恶八难处故。菩萨之人持净戒者。	持戒故則能利益一切眾生。持慈心戒。救護眾生令安樂故。持悲心戒。忍受諸苦拔[2]危難故。持喜心戒。[3]歡樂修善不懈怠故。持捨心戒。怨親平等離愛恚故。持惠施戒。教化調伏諸眾生故持忍辱戒。心常柔軟無恚[*]礙故。持精進戒。善業日增不退還故。持禪定戒。離欲不善長禪[4]支故。持智慧戒。多聞善根無厭足故。持親近善知識戒。助成菩提無上道故。持[5]遠離惡知識戒。捨離三惡八難處故。菩薩之人持淨戒者。

upholding the moral precepts, one then becomes able to benefit all beings.

When one upholds the moral precepts associated with the mind of kindness, it is for the sake of rescuing and protecting beings and causing them to be happy. When one upholds the moral precepts associated with the mind of compassion, it is for the sake of being able to endure all manner of suffering as one extricates beings from danger and difficulty.

When one upholds the moral precepts associated with sympathetic joy, it is for the sake of delighting in the cultivation of goodness and remaining free of negligence.

When one upholds the moral precepts associated with equanimity, it is in order to regard adversaries and close relations with uniform equality while abandoning both desire and hatefulness.

When one upholds the moral precepts associated with kindly giving, it is for the sake of teaching and disciplining beings.

When one upholds the moral precepts associated with patience, it is for the sake of constantly keeping the mind disposed towards pliancy and gentleness while also keeping it free of the obstacle of hatefulness.

When one upholds the moral precepts associated with vigor, it is for the sake of causing daily increase in one's good karmic deeds while preventing retreating and turning back.

When one upholds the moral precepts associated with dhyāna absorption, it is for the sake of abandoning desire and unwholesomeness while also causing growth in the branches of one's dhyāna meditation practice.

When one upholds the moral precepts associated with wisdom, it is for the sake of creating roots of goodness leading to insatiability in the pursuit of extensive learning.

When one upholds the moral precepts associated with drawing close to the good spiritual guide, it is for the sake of aiding the realization of the unsurpassed path to bodhi.

When one upholds the moral precepts associated with leaving bad spiritual guides far behind, it is for the sake of abandoning the three wretched destinies and circumstances involving the eight difficulties.[14]

E. Factors Defining "Purity in Observing Moral Precepts"

A person who is a bodhisattva is one who upholds purity in observing the moral precepts:

不依欲界不近色界不住无色界是清净戒。舍离欲尘除瞋恚[*]碍灭无明障是清净戒。离断常二边不逆因缘是清净戒。不着色受想行识假名之相是清净戒。不系于因不起诸见不住疑悔是清净戒。不住贪瞋痴三不善根是清净戒。不住我慢憍慢增上慢慢慢大慢。柔和善顺是清净戒。利衰毁誉称讥苦乐不以倾动是清净戒。不染世谛虚妄假名。顺于真谛是清净戒。不恼不热寂灭。离相是清净戒。取要言之。乃至不

简体字

不依欲界不近色界不住無色界是清淨戒。捨離欲塵除瞋恚[*]礙滅無明障是清淨戒。離斷常二邊不逆因緣是清淨戒。不著色受想行識假名之相是清淨戒。不繫於因不起諸見不住疑悔是清淨戒。不住貪瞋癡三不善根是清淨戒。不住我慢憍慢增上慢慢慢大慢。柔和善順是清淨戒。利衰毀譽稱譏苦樂不以傾動是清淨戒。不染世諦虛妄假名。順於真諦是清淨戒。不惱不熱寂滅。離相是清淨戒。取要言之。乃至不

正體字

Chapter 5: *The Perfection of Moral Virtue* 71

Not relying on the desire realm, not drawing close to the form realm and not abiding in the formless realm—these constitute "purity in observing the moral precepts."

Abandoning the objects of desire, eliminating the hindrance of hatred, and extinguishing the obstacle of ignorance—these constitute "purity in observing the moral precepts."

Abandoning the two extremes of "eternalism" and "annihilationism" while refraining from actions contradicting [the causal principles inhering in] causes and conditions—these constitute "purity in observing the moral precepts."

Not coursing in attachment to characteristics derived through false naming within the sphere of forms, feelings, perceptions, karmic formative factors, or consciousness—this constitutes "purity in observing the moral precepts."

Not being tied to causes, not formulating views, and not abiding in doubtfulness and regret—these constitute "purity in observing the moral precepts."

Not abiding in covetousness, hatred, or delusion, the three roots of unwholesomeness—this constitutes "purity in observing the moral precepts."

Not abiding in self-imputing arrogance (*asmi-māna*), elevating arrogance (*atimāna*), overweening arrogance (*māna-atimāna*), generic arrogance (*māna*), or the great arrogance (*abhi-māna*),[15] all while also remaining gentle, harmonious, and skillfully adaptive—this constitutes "purity in observing the moral precepts."

Not being even slightly moved by gain and loss, disgrace and esteem, praise and blame, or suffering and happiness—this constitutes "purity in observing the moral precepts."

Not being defiled by the false conventional designations within the sphere of worldly truth while abiding in accord with the genuine ultimate truth—this constitutes "purity in observing the moral precepts."

Abiding in quiescent cessation wherein one remains neither afflicted nor inflamed and wherein one has abandoned all phenomenal characteristics—this constitutes "purity in observing the moral precepts."

F. Summation on the Bodhisattva's Cultivation of Moral Purity

To sum up the essentials of the matter: when one continues to contemplate impermanence and continues to generate renunciation, even to the point where one refrains from cherishing his

惜身命观无常想生于厌离。勤行善根勇猛精进是清净戒。菩萨摩诃萨修行持戒不见净心。以离[6]想故。是则具足尸罗波罗蜜。	惜身命觀無常想生於厭離。勤行善根勇猛精進是清淨戒。菩薩摩訶薩修行持戒不見淨心。以離[6]想故。是則具足尸羅波羅蜜。
简体字	正體字

own physical life—when one diligently practices the development of roots of goodness and when one acts with heroic vigor—this is what constitutes "purity in observing the moral precepts."

G. THE ESSENCE OF THE BODHISATTVA'S PERFECTION OF MORAL VIRTUE

Even while the bodhisattva, *mahāsattva* cultivates the observance of the moral precepts, he does not perceive [the existence of] a "pure mind," for he has abandoned thought [prone to seizing on such characteristics]. When one accords with this, one achieves the perfection of *śīla pāramitā*.

[*]发菩提心[*]经论。

羼提波罗蜜品第六。

[0512b13] 云何菩萨修行忍辱。忍辱若为自利他利及二俱利。如是忍辱。则能庄严菩提之道。菩萨为欲调伏众生令离苦恼故修忍辱。修忍辱者。心常谦下一切众生。刚强憍慢舍而不行。见麁恶者起怜愍心。言常柔[7]濡劝化修善。能分别说瞋恚和忍果报差别。是名菩萨初忍辱心。修忍辱故。远离众恶身心安乐。是名自利。化导众生皆令和顺。是名利他。以己所修无上[8]大忍化诸众生令同己利。是名俱利。因修忍辱获得端政。人所宗敬。

简体字

[*]發菩提心[*]經論。

羼提波羅蜜品第六。

[0512b13] 云何菩薩修行忍辱。忍辱若為自利他利及二俱利。如是忍辱。則能莊嚴菩提之道。菩薩為欲調伏眾生令離苦惱故修忍辱。修忍辱者。心常謙下一切眾生。剛強憍慢捨而不行。見麁惡者起憐愍心。言常柔[7]濡勸化修善。能分別說瞋恚和忍果報差別。是名菩薩初忍辱心。修忍辱故。遠離眾惡身心安樂。是名自利。化導眾生皆令和順。是名利他。以己所修無上[8]大忍化諸眾生令同己利。是名俱利。因修忍辱獲得端政。人所宗敬。

正體字

6
Kṣānti Pāramitā

VI. CHAPTER 6: THE PERFECTION OF PATIENCE
  A. THREE KINDS OF BENEFIT AND PATH ADORNMENT FROM PATIENCE

How does the bodhisattva go about cultivating patience? If patience is cultivated for the sake of bringing about self-benefit, benefit of others, and the combined benefit of both, one becomes able thereby to adorn the path to bodhi.

  1. RIGHT MOTIVATION IN THE PRACTICE OF PATIENCE

The bodhisattva cultivates patience out of a wish to train and discipline beings in a manner whereby they are therefore caused to abandon suffering and affliction.

As for one who cultivates patience, in relating to all beings, his mind remains in a state of constant humility. Stubbornness and arrogance are relinquished and thus are not a part of his practice. When one encounters someone who is coarse and evil, he brings forth thoughts inclined towards pity. His words are always gentle, encouraging change and the cultivation of goodness. He is able to distinguish and explain the differences in the resulting retribution arising from hatefulness on the one hand and harmoniousness and patience on the other.

This is what qualifies as the mind of patience as initially cultivated by the bodhisattva.

  2. SELF BENEFIT

On account of cultivating patience, one departs far from the many sorts of evil and enjoys happiness in both body and mind. This is what is meant by "self-benefit."

  3. BENEFIT OF OTHERS

One transforms beings through teaching and guides them so that in every case they are caused to become harmonious and accommodating. This is what is meant by "benefit of others."

  4. COMBINED BENEFIT

On account of the unsurpassed great patience which one has cultivated, one teaches beings, thus causing them to gain benefit identical to one's own. This is what is meant by "combined benefit."

  5. ADORNING THE PATH OF BODHI THROUGH PATIENCE

On account of cultivating patience, one gains a body possessed of a fine and well-formed appearance, becomes one who is revered by

乃至得佛上妙相好。是名庄严菩提之道。忍辱有三。谓身口意。云何身忍。若他加恶侵毁挝打。乃至伤害悉能忍受。见诸众生[9]危逼恐惧。以身代之而无疲怠。是名身忍。云何口忍。若见骂者默受不报。若[10]见非理来呵嘖者。当[11]濡语附顺。若有加诬横生诽谤皆当忍受。是名口忍。云何意忍。见有瞋者心不怀恨。若有触恼其心不乱。若有讥毁心亦无怨。是名意忍。世间打者有二种。一者实。二者横。若有[12]罪过若人[13]慊疑为彼所打。自应忍受如服甘露。于彼人所应生恭敬。

others, and eventually even gains the supremely marvelous major marks and subsidiary characteristics of a buddha. This is what is meant by "adorning the path to bodhi."

B. The Three Types of Patience

Patience is of three types: physical, verbal, and mental.

1. Physical Patience

What is meant by physical patience? In an instance where someone visits evil actions on one's person by invading, wreaking destruction, seizing, striking, and even inflicting serious injury, one remains able in all such instances to patiently endure it. In an instance where one observes beings placed in danger, subjected to physical force, and afflicted with terror, one physically stands in for them and yet remains free of any weariness or indolence in doing so. This is what is meant by physical patience.

2. Verbal Patience

What is meant by verbal patience? In an instance where one encounters someone who subjects one to cursing, one remains silent and endures it without responding in kind. In an instance where one encounters someone who, with no basis in principle, scolds and rebukes, one should respond with gentle words and deferential accommodation. In an instance where someone subjects one to false accusations or arbitrary and fierce slanders, one should in all cases endure it patiently. This is what is meant by verbal patience.

3. Mental Patience

What is meant by mental patience? In an instance where one encounters someone who is angry, one's mind refrains from cherishing any enmity towards them. In an instance where one is subjected to torment, one's mind remains undisturbed. In an instance where one is subjected to ridicule and ruinous behavior, one's mind still remains free of resentment. This is what is meant by mental patience.

C. Two Types of Beatings

There are two types of circumstances in the world wherein one might be subjected to being beaten. In the case of the first, it has a real basis for its occurrence. In the case of the second, it is arbitrary and unwarranted.

In a case where one has transgressed by committing offenses and if one is then struck by someone motivated by animosity and suspicion, one should patiently endure it as if one were drinking sweet-dew ambrosia (*amṛta*). One should feel respect for that person.

简体字	正體字
所以者何。善能教诫调伏于我。令我得离诸过罪故。若横加恶伤害于我。当自思惟我今无罪。当是过去宿业所招。是亦应忍。复应思念。四大假合五众缘会谁受打者。又观前人如痴如狂。我当愍之。云何不忍。又骂者亦有二种。一实二虚。若说实者我应生惭。若说虚者无豫我事。犹如响声亦如风过无损于我。是故应忍。又瞋者亦尔。他来瞋我我当忍受。若瞋彼者。于未来世当堕恶道受大苦恼。以是因缘。我身若被斫截分离。不应生瞋。应当深观往业因缘。当修慈悲怜愍一切。如是小苦不能忍者。我即不能自调伏心。云何当能调伏众生。令得解脱一切恶法成无上果。	所以者何。善能教誡調伏於我。令我得離諸過罪故。若橫加惡傷害於我。當自思惟我今無罪。當是過去宿業所招。是亦應忍。復應思念。四大假合五眾緣會誰受打者。又觀前人如癡如狂。我當愍之。云何不忍。又罵者亦有二種。一實二虛。若說實者我應生慚。若說虛者無豫我事。猶如響聲亦如風過無損於我。是故應忍。又瞋者亦爾。他來瞋我我當忍受。若瞋彼者。於未來世當墮惡道受大苦惱。以是因緣。我身若被斫截分離。不應生瞋。應當深觀往業因緣。當修慈悲憐愍一切。如是小苦不能忍者。我即不能自調伏心。云何當能調伏眾生。令得解脫一切惡法成無上果。

Why? "Because he is well able to instruct, warn, train, and subdue me, thus causing me to abandon all manner of transgressions."

In a case where I am arbitrarily subjected to evil actions which inflict injury on me, I should reflect thus: "I am not now guilty of having committed any offenses. It must be then that this is a circumstance brought on by previous-life karma from the past." This, too, is something with which one should be patient.

One should also reflect thus: "In this circumstance consisting of an artificial conjunction of the four great elements and a meeting together of conditions associated with the five aggregates, just who is it that is undergoing a beating here?"

Additionally, one may contemplate the person before him as if he were mentally deranged or as if he were crazed, and reflect, "I should pity him. How could I not be patient?"

D. Two Types of Scoldings

Scoldings are also of two different types: first, those which are based on the truth; and second, those which are based on what is false. In the case of those where what is said is true, I should bring forth a sense of shame. In a case where what is said is false, it is a circumstance which has nothing to do with me. It is comparable then to the sounds of an echo and is also comparable to the sound of the passing wind which does me no harm. Therefore one should be patient in these situations.

E. The Necessity of Patience When Subjected to Others' Hatred

Again, in a circumstance involving someone who is possessed by hatred, it is just the same. In a situation where another person comes and expresses hatred towards me, I should patiently endure it. If I react with hatred towards him, then in a future lifetime, I may fall down into the wretched destinies and be forced to undergo great suffering and affliction therein. Because of such causal circumstances as these, even if my body were to be hacked up and scattered about, I still should not generate any hatred. One should deeply contemplate the nature of one's past-life karmic causes and conditions. Then one should cultivate kindness, compassion, and pity for everyone.

[One reflects], "If I cannot endure even such minor sufferings as these, I shall not even be able to train and discipline my own mind. This being so, how could I ever be able to train and discipline other beings, causing them to become liberated from all evil dharmas and causing them to perfect the unsurpassed fruition [of the Path]?"

简体字	正體字
若有智人乐修忍辱。是人[14]常得颜貌端正多饶财宝。人见欢喜敬仰伏从。复当观察。若人形残颜色丑恶。诸根不具乏于财物。当知皆是瞋因缘得。以是因缘。智者应当深修忍辱。生忍因缘有十事。一者不观于我及我所相。二者不念种姓。三者破除憍慢。四者恶来不报。五者观无常[*]想。六者修于慈悲。七者心不放逸。八者舍于饥渴苦乐等事。九者断除瞋恚。十者修习智慧。若人能成如是十事。当知是人能修于忍。菩萨摩诃萨修于清净毕竟忍时。若入空无相无愿无作。不与见觉愿作和合。不[15]猗着空无相无愿无作。是诸见觉愿作皆空。	若有智人樂修忍辱。是人[14]常得顏貌端正多饒財寶。人見歡喜敬仰伏從。復當觀察。若人形殘顏色醜惡。諸根不具乏於財物。當知皆是瞋因緣得。以是因緣。智者應當深修忍辱。生忍因緣有十事。一者不觀於我及我所相。二者不念種姓。三者破除憍慢。四者惡來不報。五者觀無常[*]想。六者修於慈悲。七者心不放逸。八者捨於飢渴苦樂等事。九者斷除瞋恚。十者修習智慧。若人能成如是十事。當知是人能修於忍。菩薩摩訶薩修於清淨畢竟忍時。若入空無相無願無作。不與見覺願作和合。不[15]猗著空無相無願無作。是諸見覺願作皆空。

Chapter 6: *The Perfection of Patience*

F. Retributions Corresponding to Presence or Absence of Patience

In a circumstance where there is a wise person delighting in the cultivation of patience, this person will always be reborn with a well-formed and attractive appearance and will always be abundantly endowed with material wealth and jewels. When people lay eyes upon him, they become delighted, respectful, deferential, and accommodating.

One should also contemplate those circumstance where a person possesses a deformed body, an ugly countenance, incomplete faculties, or a dearth of material wealth. One should realize that these effects are all obtained through causes and conditions associated with hatred.

G. Ten Bases for Developing Patience

For these reasons, the wise should deeply cultivate patience. There are ten circumstances reflecting the causes and conditions conducive to the development of patience:

First, one does not indulge a regard for the marks associated with "I" or "mine."

Second, one does not bear in mind matters of caste;

Third, one does away with arrogance.

Fourth, if one is wronged, he does not respond in kind.

Fifth, one contemplates the reflection on impermanence.

Sixth, one cultivates kindness and compassion.

Seventh, one's mind remains free of negligence.

Eighth, one maintains equanimity even in circumstances involving hunger, thirst, suffering, happiness, and such.

Ninth, one cuts off hatefulness;

Tenth, one cultivates wisdom.

If a person is able to succeed in these ten endeavors, one should realize that this person is able to cultivate patience.

H. Qualifications Prerequisite to Pure and Ultimate Patience

When the bodhisattva, *mahāsattva* cultivates pure, ultimate patience, on entering emptiness, signlessness, wishlessness, and effortlessness, he does not associate himself with view-ridden ideation, wishfulness, or artificially effortful endeavors, nor does he indulge in any attachment to emptiness, signlessness, wishlessness, or effortlessness. All such view-ridden ideation, wishfulness, and artificially effortful endeavors are empty of inherent existence.

如是忍者是无二相。是名清净毕竟忍也。若入尽结若入寂灭。不与[p513n01]结生死[2]合。不[*]猗尽结寂灭诸结生死皆空。如是忍者是无二相。是名清净毕竟忍也。若性不自生。不从他生。不和合生。亦无有出不可破坏。不可坏者是不可尽。如是忍者是无二相。是名清净毕竟忍也。无作非作无所[*]猗着。无分别无庄严。无修治无发进。终不造生。如是忍者是无生忍。如是菩萨修行是[3]忍。得受记忍。菩萨摩诃萨修行忍辱性相尽空。无众生故。是则具足羼提波罗蜜。

发菩提心[*]经论卷上。

如是忍者是無二相。是名清淨畢竟忍也。若入盡結若入寂滅。不與[p513n01]結生死[2]合。不[*]猗盡結寂滅諸結生死皆空。如是忍者是無二相。是名清淨畢竟忍也。若性不自生。不從他生。不和合生。亦無有出不可破壞。不可壞者是不可盡。如是忍者是無二相。是名清淨畢竟忍也。無作非作無所[*]猗著。無分別無莊嚴。無修治無發進。終不造生。如是忍者是無生忍。如是菩薩修行是[3]忍。得受記忍。菩薩摩訶薩修行忍辱性相盡空。無眾生故。是則具足羼提波羅蜜。

發菩提心[*]經論卷上。

简体字　　　　　　　　　　　正體字

Patience of this sort is free of any duality-based aspects. It is this which qualifies as pure and ultimate patience.

Where one enters a state characterized by the ending of the fetters or enters a state characterized by quiescent cessation, one does not associate with the fetters or birth-and-death. Neither does one indulge in the utter ending of the fetters or in the abidance in quiescent cessation. Still, the fetters and birth-and-death are in all cases [realized as] empty of inherent existence. Patience of this sort is free of any duality-based aspects. It is this which qualifies as pure and ultimate patience.

If by their very nature, [the fetters] are not self-generated, are not other-generated, and are not generated from a combination of the two, then they do not have any coming forth [into existence] either and hence are not such as can be destroyed. Whatsoever is indestructible is not susceptible to being made to come to an utter end. Patience of this sort is free of any duality-based aspects. It is this which qualifies as pure and ultimate patience.

I. Summation on the Bodhisattva's Cultivation of Patience

One does not indulge any attachment to freedom from artificially effortful endeavors or non-endeavoring. One remains free of thought inclined toward making discriminating distinctions while also being free of [any concept of] pursuing the adornment [of buddhalands]. One has no [concept of] "engaging in cultivation" or of "progressing" [on the Path]. To the very end, one does not create or produce anything at all.

Patience of this sort is the unproduced-dharmas patience. When a bodhisattva of this sort cultivates this sort of patience he realizes that patience through one receives the prediction [of definite eventual buddhahood].

J. The Essence of the Bodhisattva's Perfection of Patience

When the bodhisattva, *mahāsattva* cultivates patience, both nature and phenomenal characteristics are all realized as entirely empty of any inherent existence. It is through realizing that "beings" do not exist at all that one achieves *kṣānti pāramitā* (the perfection of patience).

发菩提心[*]经论卷下。

[*]天亲菩萨造。

[*]后秦龟兹国三藏鸠摩罗什译。

毘梨耶波罗蜜品第七。

[0513a20] 云何菩萨修行精进。精进若为自利他利及二俱利。如是精进。则能庄严菩提之道。菩萨为欲调伏众生令离苦恼故修精进。修精进者于一切时常勤[4]修集清净梵行。舍离怠慢心不放逸。于诸艰难不饶益事。心常精勤终不退没。是名菩萨初精进心。修精进故。能得世间出世间上妙善法。是名自利。教化众生令勤修善。是名利他。以己所修菩提正因。化诸众生令同己利。是名俱利。因修精进。获得转胜清净妙果。超越诸地乃至速成正觉。是名庄严菩提之道。

7
Vīrya Pāramitā

VII.Chapter 7: The Perfection of Vigor
  A. Three Kinds of Benefit and Path Adornment from Vigor

How does the bodhisattva go about cultivating vigor? If vigor is cultivated for the sake of bringing about self-benefit, benefit of others, and the combined benefit of both, one becomes able thereby to adorn the path to bodhi.

  1. Right Motivation in the Practice of Vigor

In his cultivation of vigor, the bodhisattva is motivated by a wish to so train and discipline beings that they are caused to abandon suffering and affliction.

One who cultivates vigor is diligent at all times in cultivating the accumulation of practices associated with the pure brahmin conduct[16] and in abandoning laziness and refraining from negligence. One's mind remains constantly vigorous and diligent and never retreats or sinks away even in the midst of endeavors which are freighted with difficulty and which yield one no [personal] benefits. This is what qualifies as the mind of vigor as initially cultivated by the bodhisattva.

  2. Self-Benefit

On account of cultivating vigor, one becomes able to gain the supremely marvelous and good worldly and transcendental dharmas. This is what is meant by "self-benefit."

  3. Benefit of Others

One teaches and transforms beings in a way which causes them to take up the diligent cultivation of goodness. This is what is meant by "benefit of others."

  4. Combined Benefit

On the basis of those right causes for bodhi which one has cultivated, one teaches beings, thus causing them to gain benefit identical to one's own. this is what is meant by "combined benefit."

  5. Adorning the Path of Bodhi through Vigor

By cultivating vigor, one gains ever more supreme, pure, and marvelous fruits [of the Path] and oversteps [bodhisattva] stages, even to the point that one succeeds in swiftly realizing the right enlightenment. This is what is meant by "adorning the path to bodhi."

简体字	正體字
精进有二种。一者为求无上道故。二者广欲拔济众苦而起精进。菩萨成就十念。乃能发心勤行精进。云何十念。一者念佛无量功德。二者念法不思议解脱。三者念僧清净无染。四者念行大慈安立众生。五者念行大悲拔济众苦。六者念正定聚劝乐修善。七者念邪定聚拔令反本。八者念诸饿鬼饥渴热恼。九者念诸畜生长受众苦。十者念诸地狱备受烧煮。菩萨如是思惟十念。三宝功德我当修集。慈悲正定	精進有二種。一者為求無上道故。二者廣欲拔濟眾苦而起精進。菩薩成就十念。乃能發心勤行精進。云何十念。一者念佛無量功德。二者念法不思議解脫。三者念僧清淨無染。四者念行大慈安立眾生。五者念行大悲拔濟眾苦。六者念正定聚勸樂修善。七者念邪定聚拔令反本。八者念諸餓鬼飢渴熱惱。九者念諸畜生長受眾苦。十者念諸地獄備受燒煮。菩薩如是思惟十念。三寶功德我當修集。慈悲正定

B. Two Types of Vigor

There are two types of vigor. The first type is that which is cultivated for the sake of seeking the unsurpassed Path. The second type is that wherein one generates vigor as a consequence of wishing to extensively extricate and rescue [beings] immersed in suffering.

C. Ten Recollections as Bases for Diligent Practice of Vigor

It is through perfecting ten recollections that one then becomes able to initiate the resolve to diligently practice vigor. What then are those ten? They are:

> First, one recollects the incalculably many meritorious qualities of the Buddhas.
> Second, one recollects the inconceivable and indescribable liberation brought about by the Dharma.
> Third, one recollects the Sangha's purity and freedom from defilements.
> Fourth, one recollects that it is through practice of the great kindness that one succeeds in establishing beings [on the Path].
> Fifth, one recollects that it is through practice of the great compassion that one extricates and rescues [beings from] the many sorts of suffering.
> Sixth, one recollects that it is the accumulation of right meditative absorptions that encourages delight in the cultivation of goodness.
> Seventh, one recollects those who are involved in the accumulation of wrong meditative absorptions and strives to extricate them [from such entrapment], thereby causing them to turn back to the original state.
> Eighth, one recollects the hunger, thirst, and fiery afflictions of the hungry ghosts.
> Ninth, one recollects the long endurance of manifold sufferings undergone by the animals.
> Tenth, one recollects the extensive experience of being roasted and boiled undergone by those residing in the hells.

The bodhisattva then contemplates these ten recollections in this manner: "I must cultivate and accumulate the meritorious qualities possessed by the Triple Jewel. I must encourage and instigate the practice kindness, compassion, and right meditative concentration.

简体字	正體字
我当劝励。邪定众生三恶道苦我当拔济。如是思惟专念不乱。日夜勤修无有休废。是名能起正念精进。菩萨精进复有四事。所谓修行四正勤道。未生恶法遮令不[5]起。已生恶法速令除断。未生善法方便令生。已生善法修满增广。菩萨如是修四正勤道而无休息。是名精进。是勤精进能坏一切诸烦恼界。增长无上菩提正因。菩萨若能受于一切身心大苦。为欲安立诸众生故而不疲惓。是名精进。菩萨远离恶时谄曲邪精进已修正精进。所谓修信施戒忍定慧慈悲喜舍。欲作已作当作。	我當勸勵。邪定眾生三惡道苦我當拔濟。如是思惟專念不亂。日夜勤修無有休廢。是名能起正念精進。菩薩精進復有四事。所謂修行四正勤道。未生惡法遮令不[5]起。已生惡法速令除斷。未生善法方便令生。已生善法修滿增廣。菩薩如是修四正勤道而無休息。是名精進。是勤精進能壞一切諸煩惱界。增長無上菩提正因。菩薩若能受於一切身心大苦。為欲安立諸眾生故而不疲惓。是名精進。菩薩遠離惡時諂曲邪精進已修正精進。所謂修信施戒忍定慧慈悲喜捨。欲作已作當作。

Chapter 7: *The Perfection of Vigor* 89

I must extricate and rescue those beings immersed in wrong meditative absorptions and those beings suffering in the three wretched rebirth destinies."

When one contemplates in this manner, one's mindfulness becomes ever more focused and undistracted. One diligently cultivates in this manner both day and night and thus remains free of any sort of relaxation or deterioration of one's efforts. It is this which qualifies one to be able to generate vigor characterized by right mindfulness.

D. THE FOUR RIGHT EFFORTS

The vigor of the bodhisattva is possessed of four additional factors. This involves the cultivation of what is referred to as "the path of the four right efforts":

> Whatsoever bad dharmas have not yet arisen—one blocks them off and does not allow them to arise.
>
> Whatsoever bad dharmas have already arisen—one swiftly causes them to be eliminated and cut off.
>
> Whatsoever good dharmas have not yet arisen—one institutes skillful means by which they are caused to arise.
>
> Whatsoever good dharmas have already arisen—one cultivates them to fullness, causing them to increase and become more expansive.

E. PRACTICE SCENARIOS EXEMPLIFYING VIGOR

When the bodhisattva cultivates the path of the four right efforts in this manner, doing so without resting, this is what qualifies as vigor. This diligent practice of vigor is able to destroy all afflicted mental states while also bringing about increase in the right causes for realization of the unsurpassed bodhi.

If the bodhisattva is able to endure all of the great sufferings which befall both body and mind, doing so out of a desire to establish beings [in the Path], and if he is able in doing so to remain free of weariness, it is this which qualifies as vigor.

Having departed far from the deceptiveness and wrongly-directed vigor typical of an evil age, the bodhisattva cultivates right vigor.

This is to say that, in cultivating faith, giving, moral virtue, patience, meditative concentration, wisdom, kindness, compassion, sympathetic joy, and equanimity, whether it be with respect to prospective endeavors, past endeavors, or current endeavors, he

简体字	正體字
至心常行[6]精进无悔。于诸善法及拔济众苦。如救头然心不退没。是名精进。菩萨虽复不惜身命。然为拔济众苦救护正法。当应爱惜。不舍威仪常修善法。修善法时心无懈怠。失身命时不舍如法。是名菩萨修菩提道勤行精进。懈怠之人不能一时一切布施。不能持戒忍于众苦勤行精进摄心念定分别善恶。是故说言六波罗蜜。因于精进而得增长。若菩萨摩诃萨精进增上。则能疾得阿耨多罗三藐三菩提。菩萨发大庄严而起精进。复有四事。一者发大庄严。二者积集勇健。三者修诸善根。四者教化众生。	至心常行[6]精進無悔。於諸善法及拔濟眾苦。如救頭然心不退沒。是名精進。菩薩雖復不惜身命。然為拔濟眾苦救護正法。當應愛惜。不捨威儀常修善法。修善法時心無懈怠。失身命時不捨如法。是名菩薩修菩提道勤行精進。懈怠之人不能一時一切布施。不能持戒忍於眾苦勤行精進攝心念定分別善惡。是故說言六波羅蜜。因於精進而得增長。若菩薩摩訶薩精進增上。則能疾得阿耨多羅三藐三菩提。菩薩發大莊嚴而起精進。復有四事。一者發大莊嚴。二者積集勇健。三者修諸善根。四者教化眾生。

constantly practices vigor with ultimate sincerity while remaining free of any sort of regret.

In his cultivation of all good dharmas and in his extrication and rescue of [beings] from the many sorts of suffering, he does so with the same urgency as someone putting out a fire in his own turban, never allowing his determination to retreat or sink away.

This is what is meant by "vigor."

F. The Bodhisattva's Stately Deportment and Alignment with Dharma

Although the bodhisattva cherishes no particular regard for his own physical life, still, for the sake of extricating beings from the many sorts of suffering and for the sake of protecting right Dharma, he should in fact retain a form of cherishing wherein he refrains from relinquishing the stately comportment [requiring perfectly appropriate behavior] while proceeding with constancy to cultivate good dharmas.

When he cultivates good dharmas, his mind remains free of indolence. Even were he to encounter a time when he might be required to sacrifice his life, still, he refrains from forsaking his conformity with Dharma. This is what is meant by the bodhisattva's diligent implementation of vigor as he pursues cultivation of the path to bodhi.

G. The Importance of Vigor to the *Pāramitās* and Buddhahood

A person who is subject to indolence remains unable to give up everything at once. He is also unable to uphold the moral precepts, maintain patience with the many sorts of suffering, diligently implement vigor, focus his thoughts in meditative concentration, or distinguish between what is good and what is bad. It is for this reason that it is said that the six *pāramitās* are able to progressively increase on account of vigor. If the vigor practiced by a bodhisattva, *mahāsattva* grows ever more superior, then he becomes able to swiftly gain realization of *anuttara-samyak-saṃbodhi*.

H. Four Factors in the Bodhisattva's Initiation of the Great Adornment

In the bodhisattva's initiation of the great adornment and in his bringing forth of vigor, there are four additional component factors:

First, he initiates the great adornment.
Second, he accumulates heroic strength.
Third, he cultivates all manner of roots of goodness.
Fourth, he teaches and transforms beings.

简体字	正體字
云何菩萨发大庄严。于诸生死心能堪忍不计劫数。于无量无边百千万亿那由他恒河沙阿僧只劫。当成佛道心不疲倦。是名不懈庄严精进。菩萨积集勇健而[7]起精进。若三千大千世界满中盛火。为见佛故为闻法故。为安止众生于善法故。要当从是火中而过。为调伏众生。心善安止于大悲中。是名勇健精进。菩萨修习善根而起精进。如所发起一切善根。悉以迴向阿耨多罗三藐三菩提。为欲成就一切智故。是名修习善根精进。菩萨教化众生而起精进。众生之性不可称计。无量无边同虚空界。菩萨立誓我当度之无有遗馀。为欲化度勤行精进。是名教化精进。取要言之。菩萨修助道功德助无上	云何菩薩發大莊嚴。於諸生死心能堪忍不計劫數。於無量無邊百千萬億那由他恒河沙阿僧祇劫。當成佛道心不疲倦。是名不懈莊嚴精進。菩薩積集勇健而[7]起精進。若三千大千世界滿中盛火。為見佛故為聞法故。為安止眾生於善法故。要當從是火中而過。為調伏眾生。心善安止於大悲中。是名勇健精進。菩薩修習善根而起精進。如所發起一切善根。悉以迴向阿耨多羅三藐三菩提。為欲成就一切智故。是名修習善根精進。菩薩教化眾生而起精進。眾生之性不可稱計。無量無邊同虛空界。菩薩立誓我當度之無有遺餘。為欲化度勤行精進。是名教化精進。取要言之。菩薩修助道功德助無上

Chapter 7: *The Perfection of Vigor*

1. THE INITIATION OF THE GREAT ADORNMENT

How is it that the bodhisattva initiates the great adornment?[17] His mind becomes able to endure the prospect of all of the births and deaths [involved on the bodhisattva path to buddhahood] and thus takes no account of the number of kalpas involved. Even the prospect of passing through boundlessly many hundreds of thousands of myriads of *koṭīs* of *nayutas* of Ganges' sands of *asaṃkhyeyas* of kalpas before being able then to perfectly realize the path to buddhahood is not such as causes his mind to become weary. This is what is referred to as the vigor wherein one is not lax in carrying on with adornment.

2. THE ACCUMULATION OF HEROIC STRENGTH

The bodhisattva accumulates heroic strength as he proceeds with bringing forth vigor. Even if the worlds of the great trichiliocosm were brimming with raging fire, still, if it were necessary to pass through this fire for the sake of being able to encounter the Buddha and hear the Dharma, for the sake of establishing beings in good dharmas, he would do just that. When he proceeds in this way for the sake of training and subduing beings and on the basis of having well established his own mind in the great compassion, this is what qualifies as heroic strength in the practice of vigor.

3. THE CULTIVATION OF ROOTS OF GOODNESS

The bodhisattva brings forth vigor in his cultivation of roots of goodness and, no matter what roots of every kind of goodness he has developed, he dedicates them all to *anuttara-samyak-saṃbodhi*, doing so for the sake of being able to perfect all-knowledge. It is this which qualifies as vigor in the cultivation of roots of goodness.

4. THE TEACHING AND TRANSFORMING OF BEINGS

As the bodhisattva teaches and transforms beings, he brings forth vigor. The nature of beings is that they are inestimably many. In number they are as immeasurable and boundless as empty space itself. Still, the bodhisattva establishes a vow: "I shall bring them all without exception across to liberation." For the sake of transforming them and bringing them across to liberation, he is diligent in his practice of vigor. It is this which qualifies as vigor in teaching and transforming beings.

I. SUMMATION ON VIGOR

To speak of the essentials, the bodhisattva cultivates the path-provision of merit in support of his development of unsurpassable

智慧。修集佛法而起精进。[8]诸佛功德无量无边。菩萨摩诃萨发大庄严所行精进亦复如是无量无边。菩萨摩诃萨修行精进无离欲心。拔众苦故。是则具足毘梨耶波罗蜜。	智慧。修集佛法而起精進。[8]諸佛功德無量無邊。菩薩摩訶薩發大莊嚴所行精進亦復如是無量無邊。菩薩摩訶薩修行精進無離欲心。拔眾苦故。是則具足毘梨耶波羅蜜。
简体字	正體字

wisdom. In his cultivation and accumulation of these dharmas essential to buddhahood, he brings forth vigor. The merit of the Buddhas is incalculable and boundless. The vigor practiced by the bodhisattva, *mahāsattva* as he proceeds with the great adornment is incalculable and boundless in just this same way.

J. THE ESSENCE OF THE BODHISATTVA'S PERFECTION OF VIGOR

In the bodhisattva, *mahāsattva's* cultivation of vigor, his mind is not such as abandons zeal. This is because he proceeds with extricating beings from the many sorts of sufferings. It is this then which brings about perfection of *vīrya pāramitā*.

[9]发菩提心[10]经论。

禅[11]那波罗蜜品第八。

[0513c24] 云何菩萨修习禅定。禅定若为自利他利及二俱利。如是禅定。则能庄严菩提之道。菩萨为欲调伏众生令离苦恼故修禅定。修禅定者。善摄其心。一切乱想不令妄干。行住坐卧系念在前。逆顺观察髑髅[12]顶脊臂肘胸胁髋髀。胫踝安般数息。是名菩萨初修定心。修禅定故。不受众恶心常悦乐。是名[p514n01]自利。教化众生令修正念。是名利他。以己所修清净三昧离恶觉观。化诸众生令同己利。是名俱利。

简体字

[9]發菩提心[10]經論。

禪[11]那波羅蜜品第八。

[0513c24] 云何菩薩修習禪定。禪定若為自利他利及二俱利。如是禪定。則能莊嚴菩提之道。菩薩為欲調伏眾生令離苦惱故修禪定。修禪定者。善攝其心。一切亂想不令妄干。行住坐臥係念在前。逆順觀察髑髏[12]頂脊臂肘胸脇髖髀。脛踝安般數息。是名菩薩初修定心。修禪定故。不受眾惡心常悅樂。是名[p514n01]自利。教化眾生令修正念。是名利他。以己所修清淨三昧離惡覺觀。化諸眾生令同己利。是名俱利。

正體字

8
Dhyāna Pāramitā

VIII. CHAPTER 8: THE PERFECTION OF DHYĀNA MEDITATION
A. THREE KINDS OF BENEFIT AND PATH ADORNMENT FROM DHYĀNA

How does the bodhisattva go about cultivating dhyāna absorption? If dhyāna absorption is cultivated for the sake of bringing about self-benefit, benefit of others, and the combined benefit of both, one then becomes able to adorn the path to bodhi.

1. RIGHT MOTIVATION IN THE PRACTICE OF DHYĀNA

In his cultivation of dhyāna absorption, the bodhisattva is motivated by a wish to so train and discipline beings that they are caused to abandon suffering and affliction.

One who cultivates dhyāna absorption skillfully focuses his mind and does not allow any distracted thoughts to interfere through the introduction of what is false. When walking, standing, sitting, and lying down, one's mindfulness remains anchored directly before one. Both upwards and downwards, one contemplates [the skeleton], tracing from the top of the skull on down through the spine, tracing from the upper arm bones on through the elbows [and so forth], tracing from the chest on through the rib bones, and tracing from the pelvic bones on through the shin bones, the anklebones, [and so forth]. And counting the breaths, one cultivates *ānāpāna*. This is what qualifies as the mind of meditative absorption as initially cultivated by the bodhisattva.

2. SELF-BENEFIT

On account of cultivating dhyāna absorption, one does not indulge the many sorts of evil thought, but rather always experiences blissfulness. This is what is meant by "self-benefit."

3. BENEFIT OF OTHERS

One teaches and transforms beings, causing them to cultivate right mindfulness. This is what is meant by "benefit of others."

4. COMBINED BENEFIT

On the basis of that pure samādhi which one has cultivated, that which abandons evil ideation (*vitarka*) and mental discursion (*vicāra*), one teaches beings, thus causing them to gain benefit identical to one's own. This is what is meant by "combined benefit."

简体字	正體字
因修禅定。获得八解乃至首楞严金刚三昧。是名庄严菩提之道。禅定由三法生。云何为三。一从闻慧。二从思慧。三从修慧。从是三法渐渐而生一切三昧。云何闻慧。如所闻法心常爱乐。复作是念。无碍解脱等诸佛法。要因多闻而得成就。作是念已。于一切求法时转加精勤。日夜常乐听法无有厌足。是名闻慧。云何思慧。思念观察一切有为法如实相。所谓无常苦空无我不净。念念生灭不久败坏。而诸众生忧悲苦恼憎爱所系。但为贪恚痴火所然。增长后世苦恼大聚。无有实性犹如幻化。	因修禪定。獲得八解乃至首楞嚴金剛三昧。是名莊嚴菩提之道。禪定由三法生。云何為三。一從聞慧。二從思慧。三從修慧。從是三法漸漸而生一切三昧。云何聞慧。如所聞法心常愛樂。復作是念。無礙解脫等諸佛法。要因多聞而得成就。作是念已。於一切求法時轉加精勤。日夜常樂聽法無有厭足。是名聞慧。云何思慧。思念觀察一切有為法如實相。所謂無常苦空無我不淨。念念生滅不久敗壞。而諸眾生憂悲苦惱憎愛所繫。但為貪恚癡火所然。增長後世苦惱大聚。無有實性猶如幻化。

5. Adorning the Path of Bodhi through Dhyāna

On account of cultivating dhyāna absorption, one gains realization of the eight liberations and so forth until we come to the *śūraṅgama* and *vajra* samādhis. This is what is meant by "adorning the path to bodhi."

B. The Three Dharmas from which Dhyāna Absorption Arises

Dhyāna absorption arises from three dharmas. What are those three? They are:

First, it arises from learning-derived wisdom (*śruta-maya*).

Second, it arises from deliberation-derived wisdom (*cinta-maya*).

Third, it arises from meditation-derived wisdom (*bhāvanā-maya*).

These three dharmas gradually produce all of the samādhis.

1. Learning-Derived Wisdom

What is meant by "learning-derived wisdom" (*śruta-maya*)? In accordance with whatsoever dharma one has heard, one's mind always relates to it with fondness and happiness. One additionally thinks, "Such dharmas of the Buddha as the uninterrupted path (*ānantarya-mārga*) and the path of liberation (*vimukti-mārga*) must be perfected on the basis of abundant learning." Having had this thought, whenever the opportunity arises to seek out the Dharma, one increases the intensity of his vigor so that, day and night, he always delights in tirelessly listening to the Dharma. This is what is meant by "learning-derived wisdom."

2. Deliberation-Derived Wisdom

What then is meant by "deliberation-derived wisdom" (*cinta-maya*)? One ponders and analytically contemplates all conditioned dharmas in accordance with their true character. This refers to [contemplating]: "They are impermanent, conduce to suffering, are empty, are devoid of self, are impure, are produced and cease in each successive thought-moment (*kṣaṇa-kṣaṇa-utpanna-niruddha*), and are bound to undergo ruination before long. Beings are bound up in worry, lamentation, suffering, affliction, detestation and affection. [Their existence] is solely a matter of being burned up by the fire of covetousness, hatred, and delusion while increasing the great accumulation of suffering to be undergone in later existences. [Conditioned dharmas] have no reality-based nature and are analogous to a magically-conjured illusion or a supernatural transformation."

見如是已。於一切有為法即生厭離。轉加精勤趣佛智慧。思惟如來智慧不可思議不可稱量。有大勢力無能勝者。能至無畏安隱大城不復轉還。能救無量苦惱眾生。如是知見佛無量智。見有為法無量苦惱。志願進求無上大乘。是名思慧。云何修慧。從初骨觀乃至阿耨多羅三藐三菩提。皆名修慧。離欲不善法。有覺有觀離生喜樂入初禪。滅覺觀內清淨心一處。無覺無觀定生喜樂入二禪。離喜故行捨。心念安慧身受樂。諸賢聖能說能捨。常念受樂入三禪。斷苦斷樂故。先滅憂喜故。不

Having made such observations as these, one straightaway generates renunciation for all conditioned dharmas and, with ever increasing intensity, diligently proceeds to pursue the wisdom of the Buddha. One deliberates further and realizes that the wisdom of the Tathāgata is inconceivable, ineffable, and incalculable, is possessed of great power, is unconquerable, is able to transport one to the great city of fearlessness and safety, is not such as can be turned back, and is able to rescue countless suffering and afflicted beings.

One develops such knowledge and vision regarding the immeasurable wisdom of the Buddha, perceives that conditioned dharmas are freighted with an incalculable amount of suffering and affliction, and resolves then to advance, seeking to [cultivate according to] the unsurpassed Great Vehicle. This is what is meant by "deliberation-derived wisdom."

3. Meditation-Derived Wisdom

What is meant by "meditation-derived wisdom" (bhāvanā-maya)? All [meditation practice occurring] from the initial meditative contemplation of the skeleton on through to anuttara-samyak-saṃbodhi falls into the category of "meditation-derived wisdom."

Leaving behind desire and unwholesome dharmas, still retaining "ideation" (vitarka) and "mental discursion" (vicāra), and experiencing the "joy" (prīti) and "bliss" (prasrabdhi-sukha) born of abandonment, one enters the first dhyāna.[18]

One then causes the cessation of ideation and mental discursion, abides in "inward purity" (adhyātma-saṃprasāda), and "focuses the mind in a single place" (citta-eka-agratā). Free of ideation and mental discursion, and experiencing the "joy" and "bliss" born of concentration, one enters the second dhyāna.

On account of leaving behind joy (prīti), one experiences "equanimity in the sphere of the formative-factors aggregate" (saṃskāra-upekṣa), one's mind abides in "mindfulness" (smṛti), one is established in "discerning knowing" (samprajñāna), and one experiences "physically-based bliss" (sukhā-vedanā) of the sort which āryas are able to acquire while still maintaining equanimity towards it.[19] In a state of "meditative stabilization" (sthiti, or samādhi) (lit. "constant mindfulness") and experiencing feeling-based bliss, one enters the third dhyāna.

On account of having cut off suffering and having cut off bliss—this on the basis of having earlier caused the cessation of distress and joy—abiding in "a state wherein one feels neither suffering nor

苦不乐行舍念净入四禅。过一切色相。灭一切有对相。不念一切别异相故。知无边虚空。即入虚空无色定处。过一切虚空相。知无[2]边识。即入无色识定处。过一切识相。知无所有。即入无所有无色定处。过一切无所有处。知非有想非无想。安隐即入无色非有想非无想处。但随顺诸法行故而不乐著。求无上乘成最正觉是名修慧。菩萨从是闻思修慧。精勤摄心。则能成就通明三昧禅[3]那波罗[4]蜜。

[0514b07] 复次。菩萨修定。复有十法行。不与声闻辟支佛共。何等十。

简体字

苦不樂行捨念淨入四禪。過一切色相。滅一切有對相。不念一切別異相故。知無邊虛空。即入虛空無色定處。過一切虛空相。知無[2]邊識。即入無色識定處。過一切識相。知無所有。即入無所有無色定處。過一切無所有處。知非有想非無想。安隱即入無色非有想非無想處。但隨順諸法行故而不樂著。求無上乘成最正覺是名修慧。菩薩從是聞思修慧。精勤攝心。則能成就通明三昧禪[3]那波羅[4]蜜。

[0514b07] 復次。菩薩修定。復有十法行。不與聲聞辟支佛共。何等十。

正體字

bliss," coursing in "[pure] equanimity" (*upekṣa-pari-śuddhi*), and possessed of "mindfulness which is pure," one enters the fourth dhyāna.

On account of transcending [perception of] all aspects of physical forms, on account of causing cessation of [any perception of] duality-based characteristics (as with the subject-object duality of sense faculties versus sense objects), and on account of refraining from bearing in mind any marks of differentiation, one then comes to know the state of boundless space and straightaway enters the station of the [boundless] space formless absorption.

Having transcended all aspects of empty space, one comes to know the state of boundless consciousness and straightaway enters the station of the [boundless] consciousness formless absorption.

Having transcended all aspects of consciousness, one then comes to know the state of nothing whatsoever and straightaway enters into the formless-realm absorption known as the station of nothing whatsoever.

Having transcended the station of nothing whatsoever, one then comes to know the state of neither perception nor non-perception and then, having experienced peace and security therein, one straightaway enters the formless realm's station of neither perception nor non-perception.

Through merely acquiescing in these dharmas associated with one's practice [of these meditation states] while refraining all the while from indulging any attachment to the bliss associated with them, one [continues] to seek realization of the most supreme form of right enlightenment found in the unsurpassed vehicle.

[The above instances] exemplify what is meant by "meditation-derived wisdom" (*bhāvanā-maya*).

4. Summation on the Three Types of Wisdom from Dhyāna

Through learning-derived wisdom, deliberation-derived wisdom, and meditation-derived wisdom, the bodhisattva cultivates intense diligence in focusing the mind. He then becomes able to equip himself with the samādhis associated with the spiritual penetrations and clarities and proceeds to perfect dhyāna *pāramitā*.

C. Ten Meditation Dharmas Not in Common with the Two Vehicles

Furthermore, in the bodhisattva's cultivation of meditative absorption, there are an additional ten Dharma practices which are not held in common with either the Śrāvaka Disciples or the Pratyekabuddhas. What are those ten? They are:

简体字	正體字
一者修定无有吾我。具足如来诸禅定故。二者修定不味不着。舍离染心不求己乐故。三者修定具诸通业。为知众生诸心行故。四者修定为知众心。度脱一切诸众生故。五者修定行于大悲。断诸众生烦恼结故。六者修定诸禅三昧。善知入出过于三界故。七者修定常得自在。具足一切诸善法故。八者修定其心寂灭。胜于二乘诸禅三昧故。九者修定常入智慧过诸世间到彼岸故。十者修定能兴正法。绍隆三宝使不断绝故。如是定者。不与声闻辟支佛共。	一者修定無有吾我。具足如來諸禪定故。二者修定不味不著。捨離染心不求己樂故。三者修定具諸通業。為知眾生諸心行故。四者修定為知眾心。度脫一切諸眾生故。五者修定行於大悲。斷諸眾生煩惱結故。六者修定諸禪三昧。善知入出過於三界故。七者修定常得自在。具足一切諸善法故。八者修定其心寂滅。勝於二乘諸禪三昧故。九者修定常入智慧過諸世間到彼岸故。十者修定能興正法。紹隆三寶使不斷絕故。如是定者。不與聲聞辟支佛共。

First, in the cultivation of meditative absorption, he remains free of [attachment to] a self, this through perfecting the dhyāna absorptions of the Tathāgata.

Second, in the cultivation of meditative absorption, he refrains from indulging any enjoyment of the delectability [of their associated blisses] and refrains from becoming attached to them, this on account of renouncing and abandoning defiled thought and on account of refraining from seeking his own pleasure.

Third, in the cultivation of meditative absorption, he engages in the work necessary to develop the spiritual penetrations, this for the sake of knowing the mental activity of beings.

Fourth, in the cultivation of meditative absorption done for the sake of knowing the manifold varieties of [beings'] thoughts, it is undertaken for the purpose of bringing all beings across to liberation.

Fifth, in the cultivation of meditative absorption, he practices the great compassion, this for the sake of severing the affliction-based fetters of all beings.

Sixth, in cultivating meditative absorption, he develops a skillful understanding of how to enter and exit the dhyāna samādhis, this because he transcends the three realms.

Seventh, in cultivating meditative absorption, he always abides in a state of sovereign independence, this because he perfects all good dharmas.

Eighth, in cultivating meditative absorption, his mind abides in a state of quiescent cessation, this because [his practice] is supreme over the dhyāna samādhis of the Two Vehicles.

Ninth, in cultivating meditative absorption, he constantly enters a state governed by wisdom, this because he has transcended all worlds and has reached the "other shore" [of perfection].

Tenth, in cultivating meditative absorption, he is able to bring about the flourishing of right Dharma, this because he inherits and carries on the lineage of the Three Jewels, insuring that it will not be cut off.

Meditative absorption of these sorts is not such as is held in common with the Śrāvaka Disciples or the Pratyekabuddhas.

D. Additional Characteristics of Bodhisattva Meditation Practice

复次。为知一切众生烦恼心故。是故修集诸禅定法助成住心。令此禅定住平等心。是名为定。如是等定。则等于空无相无愿无作。空无相无愿无作等者则众生等。众生等者则诸法等。入如是等是名为定。复次。菩萨虽随世行不杂于世。舍世八法灭一切结。远离愦闹乐于独处。菩萨如是修行禅定。心安止住离世所作。复次。菩萨修定。具诸通智方便慧故。云何为通。云何为智。若见色相若闻音声。若知他心若念过去。若能遍至诸佛世界。是名为通。若知色即法性。解了音声	復次。為知一切眾生煩惱心故。是故修集諸禪定法助成住心。令此禪定住平等心。是名為定。如是等定。則等於空無相無願無作。空無相無願無作等者則眾生等。眾生等者則諸法等。入如是等是名為定。復次。菩薩雖隨世行不雜於世。捨世八法滅一切結。遠離憒鬧樂於獨處。菩薩如是修行禪定。心安止住離世所作。復次。菩薩修定。具諸通智方便慧故。云何為通。云何為智。若見色相若聞音聲。若知他心若念過去。若能遍至諸佛世界。是名為通。若知色即法性。解了音聲
简体字	正體字

Chapter 8: *The Perfection of Dhyāna Meditation*

Additionally, one cultivates and accumulates all of the dharmas of dhyāna absorption for the sake of knowing the afflicted thoughts of beings. One thus assists the development of the mind of stabilization and causes this dhyāna absorption to abide with a mind of uniformly equal regard for all. This is what is meant by meditative absorption.

If one gains meditative absorptions such as these, then this is equal to [the realization of] emptiness, signlessness, wishlessness, and effortlessness. If one has achieved the equal of emptiness, signlessness, wishlessness, and effortlessness, then one achieves uniformly equal regard for all beings. If one achieves uniformly equal regard for all beings, then one achieves the state wherein all dharmas are beheld with uniformly equal regard. When one has entered a state characterized by uniformly equal regard of this sort, then this is what is meant by meditative absorption.

Furthermore, although the bodhisattva adapts to the world as he carries on his practice, still, he does not admix it with the mundane. He relinquishes the eight worldly dharmas and brings about the cessation of the fetters. He departs far from clamorous boisterousness and takes pleasure in abiding in a place of solitude. The bodhisattva cultivates the practice of dhyāna absorption in a manner such as this. His mind becomes established in a state of stabilization and he abandons worldly endeavors.

E. Four Additional Distinctive Factors in Bodhisattva Meditation

Also, in cultivating meditative absorption, the bodhisattva does so for the sake of equipping himself with the spiritual penetrations, knowing awareness, skillful means, and wisdom. What is meant by "spiritual penetrations"? What is meant by "knowing awareness"?

1. Spiritual Penetrations

Whether it be in the sphere of seeing [even distant] characteristics of form, whether it be in the sphere of the hearing [even distant] sounds, whether it be in knowing others' thoughts, whether it be in the sphere of remembering [lifetimes already in] the past, or whether it be in the sphere of the ability to go anywhere in any buddha world, these are all subsumed in what is meant by "spiritual penetrations."

2. Knowing Awareness

Where one knows that forms are identical with the nature of dharmas, where one completely understands the [nature of] sound and the actions of the mind, where one [perceives] the quiescent cessation

简体字	正體字
心行。性相寂灭三世平等。知诸佛界同虚空相而不证灭尽。是名为智。云何方便。云何为慧。入禅定时生大慈悲不舍誓愿。心如金刚。观诸佛世界。庄严菩提道场。是名方便。其心永寂无我无众生。思惟诸法本性不乱。见诸佛界同于虚空。观所庄严同于寂灭。是名为慧。是名菩萨修行禅定通智方便[5]慧故差别。四事俱行。得近阿耨多罗三藐三菩提。菩萨摩诃萨修行禅定。无馀恶心。以不动法故。是则具足禅那波罗蜜。	心行。性相寂滅三世平等。知諸佛界同虛空相而不證滅盡。是名為智。云何方便。云何為慧。入禪定時生大慈悲不捨誓願。心如金剛。觀諸佛世界。莊嚴菩提道場。是名方便。其心永寂無我無眾生。思惟諸法本性不亂。見諸佛界同於虛空。觀所莊嚴同於寂滅。是名為慧。是名菩薩修行禪定通智方便[5]慧故差別。四事俱行。得近阿耨多羅三藐三菩提。菩薩摩訶薩修行禪定。無餘惡心。以不動法故。是則具足禪那波羅蜜。

of both nature and phenomenal characteristics, where one regards the three periods of time with uniformly equal regard, and where one knows the buddhalands as characterized by being identical to empty space and yet refrains from opting for the final realization of complete cessation, this corresponds to "knowing awareness."

3. SKILLFUL MEANS

What then is meant by "skillful means"? And what is meant by "wisdom"? Where, when entering dhyāna absorption, one brings forth the great kindness and compassion, refrains from forsaking one's vows, keeps one's mind as solid as *vajra*, contemplates all of the buddha worlds, and carries on with the adornment of the *bodhimaṇḍala*, this corresponds to "skillful means."

4. WISDOM

Where one's mind abides in eternal quiescence and remains free of [the concepts of] "self" and "beings," where one remains undistracted in one's meditation on the fundamental nature of all dharmas, where one perceives all buddha worlds as identical to empty space, and where one contemplates that whatsoever one adorns is identical to quiescent cessation,[20] this corresponds to "wisdom."

F. SUMMATION ON THE BODHISATTVA'S DISTINCTIVE MEDITATION PRACTICE

This is what is meant by the bodhisattva's being distinctly different on the basis of his exercise of spiritual penetrations, knowing awareness, skillful means, and wisdom while cultivating dhyāna absorption. Through complete practice of these four matters, one succeeds in drawing close to *anuttara-samyak-saṃbodhi*.

G. THE ESSENCE OF THE BODHISATTVA'S PERFECTION OF DHYĀNA MEDITATION

When the bodhisattva, *mahāsattva* cultivates dhyāna absorption, he remains free of any extraneous or evil thoughts. It is by resort to the dharma of remaining unmoving that one then perfects dhyāna *pāramitā*.

[*]发菩提心[*]经论。

般若波罗蜜品第九。

[0514c12] 云何菩萨修习智慧。智慧若为自利他利及二俱利。如是智慧。则能庄严菩提之道。菩萨为欲调伏众生令离苦恼故修智慧。修智慧者。悉学一切世间之事。舍贪瞋痴建立慈心。怜愍饶益一切众生。常念拔济为作将导。能分别说[6]正道邪道及善恶报。是名菩萨初智慧心。修智慧故远离无明。除烦恼障及智慧障。是名自利。教化众生令得调伏。是名利他。以己所修无上菩提。化诸众生令同己利。是名俱利。因修智慧获得初

9
Prajñā Pāramitā

IX. Chapter 9: The Perfection of Wisdom
   A. Three Kinds of Benefit and Path Adornment from Wisdom

How does the bodhisattva go about cultivating wisdom? If wisdom is cultivated for the sake of bringing about self-benefit, benefit of others, and the combined benefit of both, one becomes able thereby to adorn the path to bodhi.

    1. Right Motivation in the Practice of Wisdom

In his cultivation of wisdom, the bodhisattva is motivated by a wish to so train and discipline beings that they are caused to abandon suffering and affliction.

One who cultivates wisdom studies all aspects of worldly phenomena, abandons covetousness, hatred, and delusion, establishes himself in the mind of kindness, pities and benefits all beings, constantly bears in mind extricating and rescuing beings, serves as a guide for beings, and is able to distinguish and explain what constitutes the right path, what constitutes the erroneous path, and what constitutes the karmic retribution linked to good and bad karmic actions. This is what qualifies as the mind of wisdom as initially cultivated by the bodhisattva.

    2. Self-Benefit

On account of cultivating wisdom, one separates far from ignorance, rids oneself of the affliction-based obstacles (*kleśa-āvaraṇa*), and rids oneself of the obstacles to cognition (*jñeya-āvaraṇa*). This is what is meant by "self-benefit."

    3. Benefit of Others

One teaches and transforms beings in a manner whereby they are caused to become trained and disciplined. This is what is meant by "benefit of others."

    4. Combined Benefit

On the basis of that advancement towards the unsurpassed bodhi which one has already cultivated, one teaches beings, thus causing them to gain benefit identical to one's own. This is what is meant by "combined benefit."

    5. Adorning the Path of Bodhi through Wisdom

On account of cultivating wisdom, one gains the first [bodhisattva]

简体字	正體字
地乃至萨婆若智。是名庄严菩提之道。菩萨修行智慧。有二十心能渐建立。何谓二十。当发善欲亲近善友心。舍离憍慢不放逸心。随顺教诲乐听法心。闻法无厌善思惟心。行四梵行修正智心。观不净行生厌离心。观四真谛十六圣心。观十二因缘修明慧心。闻诸波罗蜜念欲修集心。观无常苦无我寂灭心。观空无相无愿无作心。观阴界入多过患心。降伏烦恼非伴侣心。护诸善法自伴侣心。抑制恶法令除断心。	地乃至薩婆若智。是名莊嚴菩提之道。菩薩修行智慧。有二十心能漸建立。何謂二十。當發善欲親近善友心。捨離憍慢不放逸心。隨順教誨樂聽法心。聞法無厭善思惟心。行四梵行修正智心。觀不淨行生厭離心。觀四真諦十六聖心。觀十二因緣修明慧心。聞諸波羅蜜念欲修集心。觀無常苦無我寂滅心。觀空無相無願無作心。觀陰界入多過患心。降伏煩惱非伴侶心。護諸善法自伴侶心。抑制惡法令除斷心。

Chapter 9: *The Perfection of Wisdom* 113

ground and so forth until one reaches the *sarvajñā* wisdom [of omniscience]. This is what is meant by "adorning the path to bodhi."

B. Twenty Types of Mind Key to a Bodhisattva's Wisdom Realization

In the bodhisattva's cultivation of wisdom, there are twenty kinds of mind through which he is able to gradually bring about its establishment. What are those twenty? One must generate:

1. The mind which, with wholesome motivation, seeks to draw personally close to the good spiritual guide.
2. The mind which abandons arrogance and refrains from negligence.
3. The mind which complies with teachings and delights in listening to the Dharma.
4. The mind which remains insatiable in listening to Dharma while also skillfully contemplating its meaning.
5. The mind which practices the four *brahma-vihāras* (the four immeasurable minds) and cultivates right wisdom.
6. The mind which courses in "the reflection on the unlovely" (*aśubha-saṃjñā*) and thereby generates renunciation.
7. The mind which contemplates the four truths and sixteen mind states of the ārya [in gaining "the path of seeing."]
8. The mind which contemplates the twelve causes and conditions and cultivates the [three] clarities and wisdoms.
9. The mind which listens to [teachings on] the *pāramitās* and remains mindful and zealous in cultivating them.
10. The mind which contemplates impermanence, suffering, non-self, and quiescent cessation.
11. The mind which contemplates emptiness, signlessness, wishlessness, and effortlessness.
12. The mind which contemplates the abundant faults and vulnerabilities to misfortune inhering in the aggregates, sense realms, and sense bases.
13. The mind which conquers and subdues the afflictions, and recognizes that they are not one's friends.
14. The mind which guards all good dharmas and recognizes that they are one's friends.
15. The mind which suppresses and controls bad dharmas and causes them to be cut off.

简体字	正體字
修习正法令增广心。虽修二乘常舍离心。闻菩萨藏乐奉行心。自利利他随顺增进诸善业心。持真实行求一切佛法心。复次。菩萨修行智慧。复有十法善思惟心。不与声闻辟支佛共。何谓为十。思惟分别定慧根本。思惟不舍断常二边。思惟因缘生起诸法。思惟无众生我人寿命。思惟无三世去来住法。思惟无发行而不断因果。思惟法空而[p515n01]殖善不懈。思惟无相而度众生不废。	修習正法令增廣心。雖修二乘常捨離心。聞菩薩藏樂奉行心。自利利他隨順增進諸善業心。持真實行求一切佛法心。復次。菩薩修行智慧。復有十法善思惟心。不與聲聞辟支佛共。何謂為十。思惟分別定慧根本。思惟不捨斷常二邊。思惟因緣生起諸法。思惟無眾生我人壽命。思惟無三世去來住法。思惟無發行而不斷因果。思惟法空而[p515n01]殖善不懈。思惟無相而度眾生不廢。

16. The mind which cultivates right Dharma and causes it to increase and become widespread.
17. The mind which, although it cultivates [dharmas held in common with] the Two Vehicles, constantly relinquishes and abandons [allegiance to those vehicles themselves].
18. The mind which listens to [teachings from] the treasury of bodhisattva scriptures and delights in upholding them in practice.
19. The mind which, in benefiting self and others, acquiesces in the increasing development of all forms of good karmic deeds.
20. The mind which upholds the genuine practices and seeks out all dharmas of the Buddha.

C. Ten Dharmas of Skillful Contemplation Exclusive to Bodhisattvas

Furthermore, in the bodhisattva's cultivation of wisdom, there are ten additional "dharmas of skillful contemplative thought" which are not held in common with the Śrāvaka Disciples or the Pratyekabuddhas. What are those ten? They consist of:

1. The contemplation and distinguishing of the roots of meditative absorption and wisdom.
2. The contemplation of [the faults inhering in] failing to relinquish the two extreme views of annihilationism and eternalism.
3. The contemplation of the dharmas involved in production arising through causes and conditions.
4. The contemplation of the non-existence of a being, a self, a person, or a life.
5. The contemplation of the non-existence of the dharmas of the three periods of time, whether past, future, or abiding [in the present].
6. The contemplation of the nonexistence of any implementation of action even while [the efficacy of] cause-and-effect is still not cut off.
7. The contemplation of the emptiness of dharmas while still not desisting from planting [the karmic "seeds" of] good deeds.
8. The contemplation of signlessness while still continuing to bring beings across to liberation without any deterioration in those efforts.

简体字	正體字
思惟无愿而求菩提不离。思惟无作而现受身不舍。复次。菩萨复有十二善入法门。何谓十二。善入空等三昧而不取证。善入诸禅三昧而不随禅生。善入诸通智而不证无漏法。善入内观法而不证决定。善入观一切众生空寂而不舍大慈。善入观一切众生无我而不舍大悲。善入生诸恶趣而非业故生。善入离欲而不证离欲法。善入舍所欲乐而不舍法乐。善入舍一切戏论诸觉而不舍方便诸观。善入思量有为法多过患	思惟無願而求菩提不離。思惟無作而現受身不捨。復次。菩薩復有十二善入法門。何謂十二。善入空等三昧而不取證。善入諸禪三昧而不隨禪生。善入諸通智而不證無漏法。善入內觀法而不證決定。善入觀一切眾生空寂而不捨大慈。善入觀一切眾生無我而不捨大悲。善入生諸惡趣而非業故生。善入離欲而不證離欲法。善入捨所欲樂而不捨法樂。善入捨一切戲論諸覺而不捨方便諸觀。善入思量有為法多過患

Chapter 9: *The Perfection of Wisdom* 117

9. The contemplation of wishlessness while still not abandoning the quest for bodhi.
10. The contemplation of effortlessness while still not forsaking the taking on of physical bodies [to carry out the bodhisattva's endeavors].

D. THE BODHISATTVA'S TWELVE-FOLD SKILLFUL ENTRY OF DHARMA GATEWAYS

Furthermore, the bodhisattva has an additional twelve skillful entries into Dharma gateways. What are those twelve? They are:

1. He skillfully enters the samādhis of emptiness, [signlessness, wishlessness], and so forth and yet refrains from opting to take up their complete realization.
2. He skillfully enters the dhyāna samādhis and yet does not acquiesce in taking rebirth in the dhyāna [heavens].
3. He skillfully enters the spiritual penetrations and knowledges and yet does not take up final realization of the dharma of transcending outflow impurities.
4. He skillfully enters the dharmas of inwardly-directed contemplation, yet avoids realization of the "right and definite position" (*samyaktva-niyāma*) [of the arhat which would force him into a too-early nirvāṇa].
5. He skillfully enters the contemplation of all beings as empty and quiescently still and yet still does not relinquish the great kindness.
6. He skillfully contemplates all beings as devoid of self and yet does not relinquish the great compassion.
7. He skillfully enters rebirth amidst the wretched destinies and yet it is never on account of any karmic deeds that he is therefore reborn there.
8. He skillfully enters the abandonment of desire and yet he does not take up complete realization of the dharmas by which desire is entirely abandoned.
9. He skillfully enters the renunciation of bliss associated with desire and yet does not renounce Dharma bliss.
10. He skillfully enters the relinquishing of the ideations characteristic of all frivolous discourse and yet he still does not relinquish the contemplations which are consonant with skillful means.
11. He skillfully enters the contemplation of the many faults and misfortunes inherent in conditioned dharmas and

而不舍有为。善入无为法清净远离而不住无为。菩萨能修一切善入法门。即能善解三世空无所有。若作是观。观三世空智慧力故。若于三世诸佛所种无量功德。悉以迴向无上菩提。是名菩萨善观三世方便。复次。虽见过去尽法不至未来。而常修[2]善精进不懈。观未来法虽无生出。不舍精进愿向菩提。观现在法虽念念灭。其心不忘发趣菩提。是名菩萨观三世方便。过去已灭未来未至现在不住。虽如是观心心数法生灭散坏。而常不舍聚集善根助菩提法。是名菩萨观三世方便。复次。菩萨观一切善不善我无。我实不实空不

简体字

而不捨有為。善入無為法清淨遠離而不住無為。菩薩能修一切善入法門。即能善解三世空無所有。若作是觀。觀三世空智慧力故。若於三世諸佛所種無量功德。悉以迴向無上菩提。是名菩薩善觀三世方便。復次。雖見過去盡法不至未來。而常修[2]善精進不懈。觀未來法雖無生出。不捨精進願向菩提。觀現在法雖念念滅。其心不忘發趣菩提。是名菩薩觀三世方便。過去已滅未來未至現在不住。雖如是觀心心數法生滅散壞。而常不捨聚集善根助菩提法。是名菩薩觀三世方便。復次。菩薩觀一切善不善我無。我實不實空不

正體字

yet he still does not abandon the realm of conditioned [dharmas].

12. He skillfully enters the purity and far-reaching transcendence of unconditioned dharmas and yet he still does not take up residence in the unconditioned.

 E. THE BODHISATTVA'S CONTEMPLATION OF THE THREE PERIODS OF TIME

Even while the bodhisattva is able to engage in cultivating all good gateways into the Dharma, he is simultaneously able to well comprehend that the three periods of time are empty and devoid of inherent existence]. Where one [successfully] carries out this contemplation, it is through the power of that wisdom which contemplates the emptiness of the three periods of time. In a case where one dedicates to unexcelled bodhi [the merit from rejoicing in and emulating] all of the incalculable merit created by all buddhas of the three periods of time, this qualifies as the bodhisattva's skillful means in well contemplating the three periods of time.

Additionally, although one perceives that those dharmas of the past which have already come to an end do not extend into the future, still, one constantly cultivates goodness, remaining vigorous and refraining from desisting. One contemplates that although the dharmas of the future have no production by which they come into existence, still, one does not relinquish one's practice of vigor and vows to go forth toward bodhi. One contemplates that, although the dharmas of the present are newly destroyed in each successive thought-moment, still, one's mind refrains from neglecting them and thus one nonetheless sets out toward bodhi. This is what is meant by the bodhisattva's skillful means in contemplating the three periods of time.

As for what is in the past, it has already been destroyed. As for what is in the future, it has not yet arrived. As for what is in the present, it does not abide. Although one contemplates in this manner the production, destruction, scattering, and demolition of mind dharmas and dharmas belonging to the mind, one nonetheless remains constant in not relinquishing the accumulation of roots of goodness and the accumulation of dharmas assisting realization of bodhi. This is what is meant by the bodhisattva's skillful means in contemplating the three periods of time.

 F. SUMMATION ON THE BODHISATTVA'S WISDOM-BASED CONTEMPLATION

Additionally, the bodhisattva contemplates all [dharmas]: good and not good, self and non-self, real and unreal, empty and non-

简体字	正體字
空。世谛真谛正定邪定。有为无为有漏无漏。黑法白法生死涅盘。如法界性一相无相此中无法可名无相。亦无有法以为无相。是则名为一切法印不可坏印。于是印中亦无印相。是名真实智慧方便般若波罗蜜。发菩提心菩萨摩诃萨。应如是学。应如是行。如是行者即近阿耨多罗三藐三菩提。菩萨摩诃萨修行智慧心无所行。法性净故。是则具足般若波罗蜜。	空。世諦真諦正定邪定。有為無為有漏無漏。黑法白法生死涅槃。如法界性一相無相此中無法可名無相。亦無有法以為無相。是則名為一切法印不可壞印。於是印中亦無印相。是名真實智慧方便般若波羅蜜。發菩提心菩薩摩訶薩。應如是學。應如是行。如是行者即近阿耨多羅三藐三菩提。菩薩摩訶薩修行智慧心無所行。法性淨故。是則具足般若波羅蜜。

empty, worldly truth and ultimate truth, right meditative absorption and wrong meditative absorption, the conditioned and the unconditioned, outflow impurities and absence of outflow impurities, "black" dharmas and "white" dharmas, birth-and-death and nirvāṇa—he contemplates them all as being like the very nature of the Dharma realm, as being of but a singular characteristic, [that is to say], as being signless. Among all of these, there does not exist any dharma known as "signlessness," nor does there exist any inherently-existent dharma which might be deemed signless. This then qualifies as the imprint of all dharmas, the indestructible imprint. Even within this "imprint" there is no characteristic of any "imprint." This constitutes the *prajñā pāramitā* as manifest in the skillful means arising from genuine wisdom.

The bodhisattva, *mahāsattva* should train in this manner and should practice in this manner. One who practices in this manner straightaway draws close to *anuttara-samyak-saṃbodhi*.

G. THE ESSENCE OF THE BODHISATTVA'S PERFECTION OF WISDOM

Even as the bodhisattva, *mahāsattva* cultivates wisdom, his mind remains free of anything being practiced, this because the very nature of dharmas is itself pure. This then constitutes the basis by which one perfects *prajñā pāramitā*.

[*]發菩提心[*]經論。

如實法門品第十。

[0515b14] 若善男子善女人。修習六波羅蜜。求阿耨多羅三藐三菩提者。應離七法。何等為七。一者離惡知識。惡知識者。所謂教人捨離上信上欲上精進集眾雜行。二者離於女色。貪著嗜欲。狎習世人而與執事。三者離於惡覺。自觀形容貪惜愛重。染著守護謂可久保。四者離於瞋恚暴慢嫉忌。興起諍訟壞亂善心。五者離於放逸憍慢懈怠。自恃小善輕蔑於人。六者離於外道書論及世俗文頌綺飾言辭。非佛所說不應讚誦。七者不應親近邪見惡見。如是七法所應遠離。如來說言。不見更有餘法深障佛道。如此七法是故菩薩應當遠離。

10

The Dharma Gateway of Accordance with Reality

X. CHAPTER 10: THE DHARMA GATEWAY OF ACCORDANCE WITH REALITY
   A. SEVEN DHARMAS TO BE ABANDONED

If there be sons or daughters of good family who cultivate the six *pāramitās* and thereby seek *anuttara-samyak-saṃbodhi*, they should abandon seven dharmas. What are those seven? They are:

First, one abandons the bad spiritual guide. As for the "bad spiritual guide," this refers to one who instructs people to relinquish superior faith, superior zeal, and superior vigor while instructing them to accumulate many different miscellaneous practices.

Second, one abandons [lust for] the female form, covetous attachment, indulgence in desire, and the improper familiarity with worldly people whereby one pursues involvement with them.

Third, one abandons unwholesome ideation wherein one contemplates one's physical form and countenance, wherein one indulges covetous cherishing of them, wherein one esteems them with fondness, wherein one retains a defiled attachment for them, seeking to protect them, and wherein one reckons one can preserve them for a long time.

Fourth, one abandons hatred and anger, violence and arrogance, envy and jealousy, this because they promote contentiousness and disputation while corrupting and confusing the mind devoted to goodness.

Fifth, one abandons negligence, arrogance, indolence, and the reliance on minor forms of goodness as a basis for being disdainful toward others.

Sixth, one abandons non-Buddhist texts and treatises, compositions and verses devoted to worldly concerns, and artificially decorous words and phrases. One should not praise or recite anything not taught by the Buddha.

Seventh, one should not allow oneself to draw close to wrong or unwholesome views.

Dharmas such as these seven are such as one should abandon. The Tathāgata has stated, "I do not see any other dharmas aside from these which are more profoundly capable of blocking the path to buddhahood." Therefore the bodhisattva should distance himself from dharmas such as these seven.

若欲疾得无上菩提。当修七法。何谓为七。一者菩萨当亲近善知识。善知识者。所谓诸佛及诸菩萨若声闻人。能令菩萨住深法藏诸波罗蜜。亦是菩萨善知识也。二者菩萨应当亲近出家。亦当亲近阿兰若法。离于女色及诸嗜欲。不与世人而共从事。三者菩萨应当自观。形如粪土但盛臭秽。风寒热血无可贪着。日当就死宜思厌离精勤修道。四者菩萨应当常行和忍恭敬柔顺。亦劝[3]化他人令住忍中。五者菩萨应当修集精进常生惭愧。敬奉师长怜愍穷下。见[4]厄苦者以身代之。六者菩萨应当修习方等大乘诸菩萨藏。佛所赞法受持读诵。七者菩萨应当亲近修习第一义谛。所谓实相一相无相。若诸菩萨欲疾逮得无上菩提。应当亲近如是七法。

简体字

若欲疾得無上菩提。當修七法。何謂為七。一者菩薩當親近善知識。善知識者。所謂諸佛及諸菩薩若聲聞人。能令菩薩住深法藏諸波羅蜜。亦是菩薩善知識也。二者菩薩應當親近出家。亦當親近阿蘭若法。離於女色及諸嗜欲。不與世人而共從事。三者菩薩應當自觀。形如糞土但盛臭穢。風寒熱血無可貪著。日當就死宜思厭離精勤修道。四者菩薩應當常行和忍恭敬柔順。亦勸[3]化他人令住忍中。五者菩薩應當修集精進常生慚愧。敬奉師長憐愍窮下。見[4]厄苦者以身代之。六者菩薩應當修習方等大乘諸菩薩藏。佛所讚法受持讀誦。七者菩薩應當親近修習第一義諦。所謂實相一相無相。若諸菩薩欲疾逮得無上菩提。應當親近如是七法。

正體字

B. Seven Dharmas to be Cultivated

If one wishes to swiftly realize the unsurpassed bodhi, he should cultivate seven dharmas. What are those seven? They are:

First, the bodhisattva should draw personally close to the good spiritual guide. As for the "good spiritual guide," this refers to the Buddhas as well as the Bodhisattvas. In an instance where a śrāvaka disciple is able to cause a bodhisattva to abide in the treasury of profound dharmas and in the *pāramitās*, he too may serve as the good spiritual guide for a bodhisattva.

Second, the bodhisattva should draw personally close to [the dharma of] leaving behind the householder's life and he should also draw personally close to the dharma of the *araṇya* [hermitage].[21] He should abandon [lust for] the female form as well as all indulgences of desire while also refraining from participating in endeavors with worldly people.

Third, the bodhisattva should regard his own physical form as being like soil made from manure which is filled only with stinking filth and through which there courses winds, chills, heat, and blood, but which has nothing about it worthy of covetous attachment. [He should regard it as] pursuing a daily progression towards death, as suitable to be contemplated with thoughts of renunciation, and as a cause for the determination to take up intensely diligent cultivation of the Path.

Fourth, the bodhisattva should constantly practice harmonious patience, respectfulness, and gentle accommodation. He should also encourage and teach others in a way whereby they are caused to abide in patience.

Fifth, the bodhisattva should cultivate vigor, should constantly bring forth a sense of shame and a sense of blame, should respectfully serve teachers and elders, should take pity on the poverty-stricken and lowly, and should physically stand in for those he observes to be beset by hardship and suffering.

Sixth, the bodhisattva should cultivate [teachings issuing from] the Vaipulya Great Vehicle's bodhisattva treasury and should accept, uphold, study, and recite dharmas praised by the Buddha.

Seventh, the bodhisattva should draw close to and cultivate the ultimate truth, namely the true character [of dharmas], the singular character [of dharmas], and the absence of any real characteristics [in any dharma].

If bodhisattvas wish to swiftly reach realization of the unsurpassed bodhi, then they should draw close to these seven dharmas.

简体字	正體字
复次。若人发菩提心。以有所得[5]故于无量阿僧只劫。修集慈悲喜舍布施持戒忍辱精进禅定智慧。当知是人不离生死不向菩提。何以故。有所得心及诸得见。阴界入见我见人见众生见寿命见。慈悲喜舍施戒忍进定智等见。取要言之。佛法僧见及涅盘见。如是有所得见即是执着心。执着者。是名邪见。所以者何。邪见之人轮转三界永离出要。是执着者亦复如是。永离出要。终不能得阿耨多罗三藐三菩提。若人发菩提心。应当观察是心空相。何等是心。云何空相。心名意识。即是识阴意入意界。心空相者。心无心相亦无作者。何以故。是心相空无	復次。若人發菩提心。以有所得[5]故於無量阿僧祇劫。修集慈悲喜捨布施持戒忍辱精進禪定智慧。當知是人不離生死不向菩提。何以故。有所得心及諸得見。陰界入見我見人見眾生見壽命見。慈悲喜捨施戒忍進定智等見。取要言之。佛法僧見及涅槃見。如是有所得見即是執著心。執著者。是名邪見。所以者何。邪見之人輪轉三界永離出要。是執著者亦復如是。永離出要。終不能得阿耨多羅三藐三菩提。若人發菩提心。應當觀察是心空相。何等是心。云何空相。心名意識。即是識陰意入意界。心空相者。心無心相亦無作者。何以故。是心相空無

C. Bodhi Resolve's Incompatibility with "Something to be Gained"

Additionally, if a person retaining the concept of there being anything to be gained generates the bodhi resolve and then proceeds to cultivate kindness, compassion, sympathetic joy, equanimity, giving, moral virtue, patience, vigor, dhyāna absorption, and wisdom, doing so for an incalculable number of *asaṃkhyeyas* of kalpas, one should realize that, on account of retaining the concept of something to be gained, such a person will not succeed in leaving behind birth and death and will not succeed in progressing towards bodhi.

Why is this? It is on account of his retaining the thought of something to be gained as well as on account of his view conceiving the existence of attainment, his view conceiving the existence of the aggregates, sense realms, and sense bases, his view conceiving the existence of a self, his view conceiving the existence of a person, his view conceiving the existence of a being, his view conceiving the existence of a life, and his view conceiving the existence of kindness, compassion, sympathetic joy, equanimity, giving, moral virtue, patience, vigor, meditative absorption, and wisdom.

To sum up what is essential: the view conceiving the existence of the Buddha, the Dharma, and the Sangha as well as the view conceiving the existence of nirvāṇa—views such as these which conceive the existence of something to be gained are just strains of thought rooted in attachment. As for "attachment," this is what is referred to as "wrong view." Why? Persons with wrong views are those who circulate about within the three realms remaining eternally separated from the essential means of escape. This person who indulges in attachments is of just this very sort. He remains eternally separated from the essential means of escape and thus, even to the very end, remains unable to realize *anuttara-samyak-saṃbodhi*.

D. Generation of Bodhi Resolve and Contemplation of Emptiness

If a person generates the bodhi resolve, he should contemplate this mind as characterized by emptiness. What is meant by "this mind"? And what is meant by "characterized by emptiness"? "Mind" refers to the mind consciousness. It is just the mind sense base and mind sense realm subsumed within the consciousness aggregate.

As for the mind being "characterized by emptiness," the mind itself is devoid of any "mind characteristic" and is also devoid of any agent of actions. How is this the case? Any "mind characteristics" are themselves empty of any inherent existence. Nothing

简体字	正體字
有作者。无使作者。若无作者则无作相。若菩萨解了如是法者。于一切法即无执着。无执着故于诸善恶解无果报。于所习慈了无有我。于所习悲了无众生。于所习喜了无有命。于所习舍了无有人。虽行布施不见施物。虽行持戒不见净心。虽行忍辱不见众生。虽行精进无离欲心。虽行禅学无除恶心。虽行智慧心无所行。于一切缘皆是智慧。而不着智慧。不得智慧。不见智慧。行者如是修行智慧。而无所修亦无不修。为化众生现行六度而内清净。行者如是善修其心。于一念顷所种善根。福德果报无量无边。百千万亿阿僧只劫不可穷尽。自然得近阿耨多罗三藐三菩提。	有作者。無使作者。若無作者則無作相。若菩薩解了如是法者。於一切法即無執著。無執著故於諸善惡解無果報。於所習慈了無有我。於所習悲了無眾生。於所習喜了無有命。於所習捨了無有人。雖行布施不見施物。雖行持戒不見淨心。雖行忍辱不見眾生。雖行精進無離欲心。雖行禪學無除惡心。雖行智慧心無所行。於一切緣皆是智慧。而不著智慧。不得智慧。不見智慧。行者如是修行智慧。而無所修亦無不修。為化眾生現行六度而內清淨。行者如是善修其心。於一念頃所種善根。福德果報無量無邊。百千萬億阿僧祇劫不可窮盡。自然得近阿耨多羅三藐三菩提。

exists which serves as an agent of actions. Nor is there any entity which causes the initiation [and carrying out] of actions. If no agent of actions exists, then there are no [inherently existing] characteristics of the actions themselves, either.

E. THE PRACTICE OF THE BODHISATTVA WHO UNDERSTANDS EMPTINESS

If the bodhisattva completely understands dharmas of this sort, then he remains free of any attachment to any dharma. Because he is free of any attachment, he understands that no resulting karmic reward for good or bad karmic actions actually exists, understands that in the kindness which one practices, there is no self which exists at all, understands that in the compassion which one practices, there is no being which exists at all, understands that in the sympathetic joy which one practices, there is no life which exists at all, and understands that in the equanimity which one practices, there is no person which exists at all.

Although he practices giving, he does not perceive the existence of anything which is given. Although he practices the upholding of the moral prohibitions, he does not perceive the existence of a pure mind. Although he practices patience, he does not perceive the existence of any being. Although he practices vigor, no mind exists which engages in abandoning desire. Although he practices the training in dhyāna, no mind exists which engages in eliminating evil. Although he engages in the practice of wisdom, the mind nonetheless remains free of anything which is practiced.

In relation to all objective conditions, in every case he manifests wisdom and yet he does not indulge any attachment to wisdom, does not "gain" any wisdom, and does not perceive the existence of wisdom. The practitioner cultivates wisdom in this manner and yet there is nothing cultivated and nothing not cultivated. For the sake of engaging in the transformative teaching of beings, he manifests the practice of the six perfections and yet still remains inwardly pure.

F. THE FRUITS OF THIS BODHISATTVA PRACTICE

If the practitioner skillfully cultivates his mind in this way, as for those roots of goodness which he plants in just a single mind moment—the resulting rewards from such karmic blessings are incalculable and boundless, so much so that one could not come to the end of them even in a hundred thousand myriads of *koṭīs* of *asaṃkhyeyas* of kalpas. [Such a practitioner] naturally succeeds in drawing close to *anuttara-samyak-saṃbodhi*.

简体字	正體字
[*]发菩提心[*]经论。 空无相品第十一。 **[0516a10]** 往昔一时佛在迦兰陀竹林。与诸大众无量集会。尔时世尊[p516n01]斑宣正法。告诸大众。如来所说诸法无性空无所有。一切世间所难信解。何以故。色无缚无解。受想行识无缚无解。色无相离诸相。受想行识无相离诸相。色无念离诸念。受想行识无念离诸念。眼色耳声鼻香舌味身触意法亦复如是。无取无舍无垢无净。无去无来无向无背。无暗无明无痴无慧。非此岸非彼岸非中流。	[*]發菩提心[*]經論。 空無相品第十一。 **[0516a10]** 往昔一時佛在迦蘭陀竹林。與諸大眾無量集會。爾時世尊[p516n01]斑宣正法。告諸大眾。如來所說諸法無性空無所有。一切世間所難信解。何以故。色無縛無解。受想行識無縛無解。色無相離諸相。受想行識無相離諸相。色無念離諸念。受想行識無念離諸念。眼色耳聲鼻香舌味身觸意法亦復如是。無取無捨無垢無淨。無去無來無向無背。無闇無明無癡無慧。非此岸非彼岸非中流。

11

Emptiness and Signlessness

XI. CHAPTER 11: EMPTINESS AND SIGNLESSNESS
  A. AN INTRODUCTORY PASSAGE FROM SCRIPTURE:

At one time long ago, the Buddha was residing in the Karaṇḍa Veṇuvana bamboo grove together with the entire Great Assembly which was gathered together in a countless multitude. At that time, as the Bhagavān was sequentially explaining right Dharma, he told everyone in the Great Assembly:
"The dharmas proclaimed by the Tathāgata are devoid of any inherently-existent nature, are empty, and are devoid of anything whatsoever which exists therein."

  1. EXPLANATION OF THE CONCEPTS OF "EMPTINESS" AND "SIGNLESSNESS"

This is something which all inhabitants of the World find difficult to believe or understand. How is this the case? With respect to the form [aggregate], there is neither any state of being bound up nor any state of being released. Feelings, perceptions, karmic formative factors (saṃskāra), and consciousness, too, are such as do not involve either any state of being bound up or any state of being released.

Form itself is devoid of any characteristic signs and exists apart from any characteristic signs. Feelings, perceptions, karmic formative factors, and consciousness, too, are themselves devoid of any characteristic signs and exist apart from any characteristic signs.

Form itself is devoid of any thought [imputing its existence] and exists apart from any thought. Feelings, perceptions, karmic formative factors, and consciousness, too, are themselves devoid of any thought [imputing their existence] and exist apart from any thought.

The same is true for the eye and visual forms, the ear and sounds, the nose and fragrances, the tongue and flavors, the body and tangibles, and the intellectual mind and its dharmas [as objects of mind].

There is no grasping and there is no relinquishing. There is no defilement and there is no purity. There is no going and there is no coming. There is no "facing towards" and there is no "turning away." There is no darkness and there is no brightness. There is no delusion and there is no wisdom. Nor is it the case that there is any "this shore," any "other shore," or any "abiding within the flow" [of

是名无缚。无缚故空。空名无相。无相亦空。是名为空。空名无念。无念亦空。是名为空。空[2]念亦空。是名为空。空中无善无恶。乃至亦无空相。是故名空。菩萨若如是知阴界入性。即不取着。是名法忍。菩萨[3]如是忍故。得[4]授记忍。诸佛子。譬如[5]菩萨仰书虚空。悉写如来十二部经。经无量劫佛法已灭。求法之人无所见闻。众生颠倒造恶无边复有他方净智慧人。怜愍众生广求佛法。行到于此见空中字。文画分明即便识之。读诵受持如所说行。广演

简体字

是名無縛。無縛故空。空名無相。無相亦空。是名為空。空名無念。無念亦空。是名為空。空[2]念亦空。是名為空。空中無善無惡。乃至亦無空相。是故名空。菩薩若如是知陰界入性。即不取著。是名法忍。菩薩[3]如是忍故。得[4]授記忍。諸佛子。譬如[5]菩薩仰書虛空。悉寫如來十二部經。經無量劫佛法已滅。求法之人無所見聞。眾生顛倒造惡無邊復有他方淨智慧人。憐愍眾生廣求佛法。行到於此見空中字。文畫分明即便識之。讀誦受持如所說行。廣演

正體字

the river of suffering]. This is what is meant by "the nonexistence of any state of being bound up."

Because there is [in these phenomena] no state of being bound up, they are empty of any inherent existence. "Emptiness of inherent existence" is itself a reference to "signlessness." And even "signlessness" itself is empty. This is what is meant by "emptiness."

"Emptiness" is also just a reference to the absence of any thought [imputing existence]. The absence of any thought [imputing existence] is itself empty. This, too, is what is meant by "emptiness."

Any thought which even conceives of "emptiness" is itself empty. This too is what is meant by "emptiness."

In emptiness, there is no good and there is no evil, and so forth, even to the point that there does not exist any characteristic sign of emptiness either.

It is on the basis of this that one speaks of "emptiness." If a bodhisattva cognizes the nature of the aggregates, the sense realms, and the sense bases in this way, he straightaway refrains from indulging in any clinging attachment. This is what then qualifies as "patience with respect to dharmas."

Because the bodhisattva has realized this type of patience, he is able to develop that very patience which is gained at the time of the prediction [of eventual buddhahood].

2. A Comprehensive Analogy

Sons of the Buddha. By way of analogy, suppose there were a bodhisattva who, facing upwards, proceeded to write in empty space and then completely wrote out all of the twelve categories of scriptural text ever spoken by the Tathāgata. Suppose then that one then passed through countless kalpas wherein the Dharma of the Buddha so completely disappeared that persons seeking the Dharma would have no trace of it which they might either see or hear.

Suppose then that beings became so affected by inverted views that they created a boundless amount of evil karmic deeds, whereupon there came to be a wise man from some other region who, taking pity on those beings, searched widely for the Dharma of the Buddha. Next, suppose that, having traveled to this place, he observed the words written in space, noticed that the writing of the texts was distinctly clear, straightaway understood them, studied them, recited them, preserved them, cultivated them in accordance with the manner in which they were taught, extensively expounded

分别利益众生。此书空者识空字人可思议不。而得宣传修习受持。引导众生令离系缚。诸佛子。如来说言。过去世时求菩提道。得值三十三亿九万八千诸佛。尔时皆为转轮圣王。以一切乐具。供养诸佛及弟子众。以有所得故不得[*]授记。于后复值八万四千亿九万辟支佛。亦以四事尽形供养。过是[6]以后。复值六百二十万一千二百六十一佛。尔时皆为转轮圣王。以一切乐具尽形供养。诸佛灭后起七宝塔供养舍利。后佛出世奉迎劝请转正法轮。供养如是百千万亿诸佛。是诸如来皆于空法中说诸法相。以有所得故亦不得[*]授记。如是展转乃至得值然灯佛兴。见佛闻法即得一切无生法忍。

简体字

分別利益眾生。此書空者識空字人可思議不。而得宣傳修習受持。引導眾生令離繫縛。諸佛子。如來說言。過去世時求菩提道。得值三十三億九萬八千諸佛。爾時皆為轉輪聖王。以一切樂具。供養諸佛及弟子眾。以有所得故不得[*]授記。於後復值八萬四千億九萬辟支佛。亦以四事盡形供養。過是[6]以後。復值六百二十萬一千二百六十一佛。爾時皆為轉輪聖王。以一切樂具盡形供養。諸佛滅後起七寶塔供養舍利。後佛出世奉迎勸請轉正法輪。供養如是百千萬億諸佛。是諸如來皆於空法中說諸法相。以有所得故亦不得[*]授記。如是展轉乃至得值然燈佛興。見佛聞法即得一切無生法忍。

正體字

Chapter 11: *Emptiness and Signlessness*

them, made detailed distinctions regarding their meaning, and by doing so thus benefited those beings.

As for this writing in empty space and this person who recognized the words written in space—are they such as one can either conceive of or describe? And yet he did indeed succeed in proclaiming [those teachings], passed them on, cultivated them, preserved them, used them to guide forth beings, and used them to influence beings to abandon the fetters which held them in bondage.

Sons of the Buddha, the Tathāgata has stated that at a time in the past, he sought the path to bodhi and succeeded in encountering buddhas numbering thirty-three *koṭīs* plus ninety-eight thousand. During that time, he was in every case a wheel-turning sage king who, using all manner of happiness-providing accoutrements, made offerings to those buddhas and to their assemblies of disciples as well. Nonetheless, because he retained [the concept of] something which might be gained, he did not then succeed in receiving the prediction [of eventual buddhahood].

Subsequently, he additionally encountered pratyekabuddhas numbering eighty-four thousand *koṭīs* plus ninety thousand. In this case, too, he made offerings of the four requisites to the very end of each of his lives.

After this had transpired, he additionally encountered six million, two hundred and one thousand, two hundred and sixty-one more buddhas. Throughout that time, he was in every case a wheel-turning sage king who, using all manner of happiness-providing accoutrements, made offerings. After each of those buddhas had passed into cessation, he erected stupas made of the seven precious things and made offerings to their *śarīra*. Then, whenever the next buddha manifest in the World, he respectfully welcomed him, and, offering encouragements, requested him to turn the wheel of right Dharma. In this same fashion, he continued to make offerings to a hundred thousand myriads of *koṭīs* of buddhas.

All of these Tathāgatas, even in the midst of empty dharmas, described the characteristic signs of dharmas. On account of retaining the concept of something which might be gained, he still failed during that time to receive the prediction [of eventual buddhahood]. And so it continued on in this fashion until he met Burning Lamp Buddha during the time when that buddha was flourishing in the World. He met the Buddha, listened to the Dharma, and then straightaway realized the unproduced-dharmas patience. After he

得是忍已乃得[*]授記。然灯如来于空法中说诸法相。度脱无量百千众生。而无所说亦无所度。牟尼世尊兴出于世。于空法中说有文字。示教利喜普得受行。而无所示亦无受行。当[7]如是法性相尽空。书者亦空识者亦空。说者亦空解者亦空。从本来空未来亦空现在亦空。而诸菩萨积集万善方便力故。精勤不懈功德成满。得阿耨多罗三藐三菩提。此实甚难不可思议。于无法中说诸法相。于无得中说有得法。如此之事诸佛境界。以无量智乃可得解。非是思量所能得知。新发意菩萨诚心敬仰爱乐菩提。信

得是忍已乃得[*]授記。然燈如來於空法中說諸法相。度脫無量百千眾生。而無所說亦無所度。牟尼世尊興出於世。於空法中說有文字。示教利喜普得受行。而無所示亦無受行。當[7]如是法性相盡空。書者亦空識者亦空。說者亦空解者亦空。從本來空未來亦空現在亦空。而諸菩薩積集萬善方便力故。精勤不懈功德成滿。得阿耨多羅三藐三菩提。此實甚難不可思議。於無法中說諸法相。於無得中說有得法。如此之事諸佛境界。以無量智乃可得解。非是思量所能得知。新發意菩薩誠心敬仰愛樂菩提。信

简体字　　　　　　　　　正體字

had realized this patience, he then succeeded in receiving the prediction [of eventual buddhahood].

Burning Lamp Tathāgata, even in the midst of empty dharmas, described the characteristic signs of dharmas, brought across to liberation countless hundreds of thousands of beings, and yet had nothing whatsoever which he spoke and nobody whatsoever who he brought across to liberation.

When Shākyamuni Tathāgata came forth and flourished in the world, even in the midst of empty dharmas, he spoke of the existence of language and words and thereby revealed the teachings, benefited, and delighted [beings], and caused universal acceptance and practice [of those teachings]. Still, there was nothing whatsoever which he revealed, nor was there anybody whatsoever who accepted and practiced [those teachings].

Both the nature and characteristic signs of those dharmas at that time were all entirely empty [of any inherent existence]. The writing was itself empty [of any inherent existence]. And so, too, was the person recognizing them also empty [of any inherent existence]. The person explaining them was himself empty. And so, too, was anyone comprehending them also empty.

From their very origin on forward, they were all empty. So, too, are they empty in the future and so, too, are they empty in the present. Even so, the bodhisattvas continue to accumulate the myriad sorts of goodness, this on account of the power of their skillful means. They remain intensely diligent and unrelenting in their perfect fulfillment of their stock of merit and in their [progressing towards] realization of *anuttara-samyak-saṃbodhi*.

This is truly an extremely difficult endeavor which is inconceivable and indescribable: Even in the midst of nonexistent dharmas, there continues to be the description of the characteristic signs of dharmas. And even in the midst of there being nothing whatsoever to be gained, one speaks of the existence of dharmas associated with gain.

Matters of this sort are the exclusive domain of the Buddhas who, when they employ their incalculably vast wisdom, are only then able to succeed in comprehending them. This is not something one can succeed in knowing solely through contemplative thought.

B. Faith-Based Patience and its Role in Realizing Fruits of the Path

The bodhisattva who has newly generated the resolve sincerely reveres, is fond of, and delights in bodhi. Based on his faith in the

简体字	正體字
佛语故渐能得入。云何为信。信观四谛。除诸烦恼妄见结缚得阿罗汉。信观十二因缘。灭除无明生起诸行得辟支佛。信修四无量心六波罗蜜得阿耨多罗三藐三菩提。是名信忍。众生于无始生死[8]取相执着不见法性。当先观察自身五阴假名众生。是中无我无有众生。何以故。若有我者我应自在。而诸众生常为生老病死之所侵害不得自在。当知无我。无我即无作者。无作者亦无受者。法性清净如实常住。如是观察未能究竟。是名顺忍。菩萨修信顺忍已。不久当成最上法忍。	佛語故漸能得入。云何為信。信觀四諦。除諸煩惱妄見結縛得阿羅漢。信觀十二因緣。滅除無明生起諸行得辟支佛。信修四無量心六波羅蜜得阿耨多羅三藐三菩提。是名信忍。眾生於無始生死[8]取相執著不見法性。當先觀察自身五陰假名眾生。是中無我無有眾生。何以故。若有我者我應自在。而諸眾生常為生老病死之所侵害不得自在。當知無我。無我即無作者。無作者亦無受者。法性清淨如實常住。如是觀察未能究竟。是名順忍。菩薩修信順忍已。不久當成最上法忍。

Chapter 11: *Emptiness and Signlessness* 139

discourses of the Buddha, he gradually becomes able to succeed in gaining entry to it.

What then is meant by "faith"? When, equipped with faith, one contemplates the four truths, one then proceeds to eliminate the afflictions, false views, and fetters and then finally succeeds in realizing arhatship. When, equipped with faith, one contemplates the twelve causes and conditions, one proceeds to extinguish ignorance's production of actions and then finally succeeds in realizing pratyekabuddhahood. When, equipped with faith, one proceeds to cultivate the four immeasurable minds and the six *pāramitās*, one then finally succeeds in realizing *anuttara-samyak-saṃbodhi*. This is what is known as "patience rooted in faith."

C. Acquiescence-Based Patience from Partial Cognition of Non-Self

Throughout the time they have coursed in beginningless births and deaths, beings have grasped at phenomenal characteristics, have become attached, and have failed to perceive the nature of dharmas. One should first analytically contemplate one's own person as consisting of the five aggregates which are only falsely designated as constituting a "being." There is herein nothing whatsoever constituting a "self" and nothing whatsoever constituting a "being."

How is it that this is the case? If a self actually did exist, then that self should be sovereignly independent. However, beings are constantly being invaded and injured by birth, aging, sickness, and death and thus they fail to realize any sovereign independence.

One should realize that there is no self. The absence of self is just the absence of any agent of actions. Not only is there no agent of actions, there is also no one who undergoes experiences. The nature of dharmas is pure, accords with reality, and constantly abides.

When one contemplates analytically in this manner but has not yet been able to carry [such contemplations] to their most ultimate point, this is what is known as "acquiescence-based patience."

D. Supreme Patience via Faith-Based and Acquiescence-Based Patience

After the bodhisattva has cultivated both faith-based and acquiescence-based patience, it will not be long before he will also succeed in realizing the most superior form of patience with respect to dharmas.

[*]发菩提心[*]经论。
功德持品第十二。

[0516c09] 菩萨具足修无相心。而心未[9]曾住于作业。是菩萨于诸业相知而故作。为修善根求菩提故不舍有为。为诸众生修大悲故不住无为。为一切佛真妙智故不舍生死。为度无边众生令无馀故不住涅盘。是名菩萨摩诃萨深心求阿耨多罗三藐三菩提。诸佛子。菩萨成就十法。终不退失无上菩提。何谓为十。一者菩萨深发无上菩提之心。教化众生亦令发心。二者常乐见佛以己所珍奉施供养深种善根。三者为求法故以尊敬心供养法师听法无厌。四者若见比丘僧坏为二部。互起诤讼共相过恶。勤求方便令其和合。

12

On the Merit and on Preserving Dharma

XII. CHAPTER 12: ON THE MERIT AND ON PRESERVING DHARMA
   A. CHARACTERISTICS OF A BODHISATTVA'S BODHI-DIRECTED CULTIVATION

The bodhisattva perfects the cultivation of the mind cognizing signlessness and so never allows his mind to abide in the carrying out of karmic deeds. This bodhisattva realizes [the empty nature of] the characteristic signs of karmic deeds and yet still deliberately engages in performing them.

For the sake of cultivating roots of goodness and seeking bodhi, he does not relinquish involvement in the conditioned. Because he cultivates the great compassion for the sake of all beings, he does not abide in the unconditioned.

For the sake of realizing the genuine and sublime wisdom of all buddhas, he does not relinquish involvement in the sphere of birth and death. For the sake of bringing a boundless number of beings across to liberation and allowing them to reside in the remainderless [nirvāṇa], he does not himself abide in nirvāṇa.

This is what constitutes the bodhisattva, *mahāsattva's* striving with profound mind for realization of *anuttara-samyak-saṃbodhi*.

   B. TEN BODHISATTVA DHARMAS ENSURING NON-RETREAT

Sons of the Buddha. The bodhisattva perfects ten dharmas through which he never retreats from the unsurpassed bodhi. What then are those ten? They are:

First, the bodhisattva generates with profound mind the resolve to gain the unsurpassed bodhi while also teaching beings so that they, too, are then caused to generate the same resolve.

Second, he constantly delights in seeing the Buddhas, in respectfully giving offerings to them of whatsoever he most treasures, and in deeply planting roots of goodness.

Third, for the sake of seeking the Dharma, he proceeds with a reverent mind to make offerings to the masters of Dharma and to listen tirelessly to the teaching of Dharma.

Fourth, if he encounters a circumstance where the Bhikshu Sangha has broken itself into two factions involved in mutual contentiousness, accusations, and fault-finding, he diligently seeks to implement skillful means by which they are allowed to become harmoniously united again.

五者若见国土邪恶增上佛法欲坏。能读诵说乃至一偈令法不绝。专心护法不惜身命。六者见诸众生恐畏苦恼。为作救护施以无畏。七者发勤修行求如是等方等大乘甚深经法诸菩萨藏。八者得是法已受持读诵。如所说行如所说住。九者自住于法。亦能劝导令多众生入是法中。十者入法中已能为解说。示教利喜开悟众生。菩萨成就如是十法。于无上菩提终不退失。菩萨应当如是修行此经。如是经典不可思议。所谓能生一切大慈悲种。是经能开悟引导具缚众生令[p517n01]其发心。是经能为向菩提者而作生因。是经能成一切菩萨无动之行。是经能为过去未来现在诸佛之所护念。若有善男子善女人。欲勤修集无上菩提。当广宣流布如是经典。	五者若見國土邪惡增上佛法欲壞。能讀誦說乃至一偈令法不絕。專心護法不惜身命。六者見諸眾生恐畏苦惱。為作救護施以無畏。七者發勤修行求如是等方等大乘甚深經法諸菩薩藏。八者得是法已受持讀誦。如所說行如所說住。九者自住於法。亦能勸導令多眾生入是法中。十者入法中已能為解說。示教利喜開悟眾生。菩薩成就如是十法。於無上菩提終不退失。菩薩應當如是修行此經。如是經典不可思議。所謂能生一切大慈悲種。是經能開悟引導具縛眾生令[p517n01]其發心。是經能為向菩提者而作生因。是經能成一切菩薩無動之行。是經能為過去未來現在諸佛之所護念。若有善男子善女人。欲勤修集無上菩提。當廣宣流布如是經典。
简体字	正體字

Chapter 12: *On the Merit and on Preserving Dharma*

Fifth, if he encounters a circumstance of increasing perversity and evil in his country, one whereby the Dharma of the Buddha verges on falling into ruin, he is able then to read out, recite, and expound on it, even if it be but a single verse through which he prevents the Dharma from being cut off. He then dedicates himself to preserving the Dharma, even to the point where he relinquishes any cherishing regard for his own physical life.

Sixth, whenever he encounters beings beset by the suffering and the affliction of fearfulness, he acts to rescue and protect them, thus bestowing fearlessness on them.

Seventh, he initiates a diligent cultivation practice through which he seeks out such extremely profound sutra dharmas as these from the *vaipulya* Mahāyāna's treasury of bodhisattva scriptures.[22]

Eighth, after he has found such Dharma, he accepts and upholds it through study, recitation, practicing it as taught, and through abiding in a manner which accords with its dictates.

Ninth, he himself abides in the Dharma while also being able to exhort, lead, and otherwise cause a multitude of beings to enter into this Dharma.

Tenth, after they have entered into this Dharma, he develops competence in explaining it for their sakes, revealing and teaching it, benefiting and delighting them, and thereby causing those beings to awaken.

In a circumstance where the bodhisattva perfects ten dharmas of this sort, he will never retreat from the unsurpassed bodhi. The bodhisattva should cultivate this sutra in this manner.

    C. BENEFITS ARISING FROM SCRIPTURES SUCH AS THESE

Sutras such as this are inconceivable and indescribable. Specifically, they are able to produce all seeds of the great kindness and great compassion. This sutra is able to awaken, lead forth, and guide beings constrained by the fetters, influencing them to generate the resolve [to realize bodhi]. This sutra is able to act as the initiating cause for those proceeding towards bodhi. This sutra is able to establish the unmoving practice of all bodhisattvas.[23] This sutra is worthy to be one of which all buddhas of the past, future, and present are protectively mindful.

If there be a son or daughter of good family who wishes to diligently cultivate and accumulate [the provisions for] the unsurpassed bodhi, they should extensively proclaim and circulate sutras such as these, thus preventing them from being cut off in the lands of

于阎浮提使不断绝。令无量无边众生得闻是经。若有善男子善女人闻是经者。是诸人等悉得猛利不可思议大智慧聚。不可称量福德果报。所以者何。是经能开无量清净慧眼。能[2]令佛种相续不断。能救无量苦恼众生。能照一切无明痴暗。能破四魔及诸魔业。能坏一切外道邪见。能灭一切烦恼大火。能消因缘生起诸行。能断悭贪破戒瞋恚懈怠乱意愚痴六极重病能除业障报障法障烦恼障诸见障无明障智障习障。取要言之。此经能令一切恶法消灭无馀。能令一切善法炽然增长。若有善男子善女人。闻是经已。欢喜爱乐生希有心。当知是人[3]已曾供养无量诸佛深种善根。所以者何。此经是三世诸佛之所履行。是故行者得闻是经。当自庆幸获大善利。若有书写读诵此经。当知此人所获福报无量无边。所以者何。

简体字

於閻浮提使不斷絕。令無量無邊眾生得聞是經。若有善男子善女人聞是經者。是諸人等悉得猛利不可思議大智慧聚。不可稱量福德果報。所以者何。是經能開無量清淨慧眼。能[2]令佛種相續不斷。能救無量苦惱眾生。能照一切無明癡闇。能破四魔及諸魔業。能壞一切外道邪見。能滅一切煩惱大火。能消因緣生起諸行。能斷慳貪破戒瞋恚懈怠亂意愚癡六極重病能除業障報障法障煩惱障諸見障無明障智障習障。取要言之。此經能令一切惡法消滅無餘。能令一切善法熾然增長。若有善男子善女人。聞是經已。歡喜愛樂生希有心。當知是人[3]已曾供養無量諸佛深種善根。所以者何。此經是三世諸佛之所履行。是故行者得聞是經。當自慶幸獲大善利。若有書寫讀誦此經。當知此人所獲福報無量無邊。所以者何。

正體字

Chapter 12: *On the Merit and on Preserving Dharma*

Jambudvīpa, and thus causing a countless and boundless number of beings to succeed in hearing this sutra.

If there be sons or daughters of good family who succeed in hearing this sutra, persons such as these all come into possession of the accumulation of the fiercely sharp, inconceivable, and indescribable great wisdom and shall also gain an incalculably great karmic reward in the form of merit.

Why is this the case? It is because this sutra is able to open pure wisdom eyes incalculable in their number. It is able to cause the lineage of the Buddhas to continue on and not be cut off. It is able to rescue countless beings beset by suffering and affliction. It is able to illuminate the darkness of all forms of ignorance. It is able to rout the four types of demons and demolish demonic karma. It is able to destroy the erroneous views of all non-Buddhist traditions. It is able to extinguish the great blaze of all afflictions. It is able to melt away all of the karmic formative actions (*saṃskāras*) generated through [the chain of] causes and conditions.

It is able to cut off covetousness, the breaking of the moral precepts, hatred, indolence, mental distraction, and delusion, these six extremely grave disorders. It is able to eliminate karmic obstacles, retribution obstacles, obstacles to Dharma, the obstacle of afflictions, the obstacle of views, the obstacle of ignorance, obstacles to cognition, and the obstacle of habitual propensities. To sum up the essentials: This sutra is able to cause all evil dharmas without exception to be completely melted away and disappear. It is able to cause all good dharmas to increase and grow like a flaming blaze.

D. The Meritoriousness of this Sutra and Those Revering It

If there be a son or daughter of good family who, having heard this sutra, delights in it, becomes fondly pleased by it, and is inspired to thoughts admiring its rarity, one should realize that this person has already made offerings to countless buddhas and has already deeply planted roots of goodness.

How is this the case? This sutra is one which has been carried out in practice by all buddhas of the three periods of time. Hence the practitioner who succeeds in hearing this sutra should celebrate his good fortune in acquiring such a great and fine benefit.

If there be someone who writes out, studies, or recites this sutra, one should realize that the resulting merit-based blessings gained by this person are incalculable and boundless. Why is this? The objective sphere encompassed by [the teachings of] this sutra is

简体字	正體字
此经所缘无边故。兴发无量大誓愿故。摄受一切诸众生故。庄严无上大菩提故。所获福[4]报亦复如是无有限量。若能解其义趣如说修行。一切诸佛于阿僧只劫。以无尽智说其福报。亦不能尽。若有法师说是经处。当知是中便应起塔。何以故。是真实正法所出生处故。是经随在国土城邑聚落寺庙精舍。当知是中即有法身。若人供养香花伎乐悬缯幡盖歌呗赞叹合掌恭敬。当知是人已绍佛种。况复具足受持经者。是诸人等成就功德智慧庄严。于未来世当得[*]授记。决定当成阿耨多罗三藐三菩提。 发菩提心[5]经论卷下。	此經所緣無邊故。興發無量大誓願故。攝受一切諸眾生故。莊嚴無上大菩提故。所獲福[4]報亦復如是無有限量。若能解其義趣如說修行。一切諸佛於阿僧祇劫。以無盡智說其福報。亦不能盡。若有法師說是經處。當知是中便應起塔。何以故。是真實正法所出生處故。是經隨在國土城邑聚落寺廟精舍。當知是中即有法身。若人供養香花伎樂懸繒幡蓋歌唄讚歎合掌恭敬。當知是人已紹佛種。況復具足受持經者。是諸人等成就功德智慧莊嚴。於未來世當得[*]授記。決定當成阿耨多羅三藐三菩提。 發菩提心[5]經論卷下。

boundless. This is because it promotes the flourishing generation of countless vows, because it draws in all beings, and because it involves the adornment of unsurpassed bodhi. Thus the merit-based blessings gained in reward are themselves boundless in this very same way.

If one is able to comprehend its meaning and then proceed to cultivate in accordance with what it teaches, even if all buddhas attempted for *asaṃkhyeyas* of kalpas with their inexhaustible wisdom to describe the karmic rewards generated by this, not even they could come to the end of them.

If there be a place where a master of the Dharma has taught this sutra, one should realize that one should erect a stupa on this site. Why? This is because that place is one in which genuine right Dharma was brought forth.

In whatsoever place this sutra abides, whether it be a country, city, village, monastery, temple, or serene monastic abode, one should realize that the Dharma body itself abides therein. If a person makes offerings there of incense, flowers, music, hanging banners, pennants, canopies, songs, verses, praises, pressed palms, or expressions of reverence, one should realize that this person has already himself participated in the carrying on of the lineage of the Buddhas. How much the more so is this true in the case of one who in the most complete fashion upholds [the teachings of] this sutra. Persons such as these perfect the adornments consisting of merit and of wisdom. In a future life, they are bound to receive the prediction [of eventual buddhahood]. They will definitely succeed in realizing *anuttara-samyak-saṃbodhi*.

End of *A Treatise on the Generating the Bodhi Resolve Sutra*

Endnotes

1. This is work number 1659 in the *Taisho* version of the Chinese Buddhist Canon (T.32.1659.508c04-517b06).
2. The title preserved in the Taisho edition of the Chinese Buddhist canon suggests Vasubandhu's "treatise" is directly linked to a particular sutra. Repeated digital searches in the immense Chinese Buddhist canon have so far been ineffective in locating precisely which sutra may have served as the root text upon which Vasubandhu's treatise might have served as a commentary. In contrast to Taisho's titling of the text, four Chinese editions do not include titling language specifically stating Vasubandhu's work is a sutra commentary *per se*. That, said, the "treatise" does indeed betray an implicit relationship with embedded sutra or *mātṛkā*-treasury text while, thankfully, still standing quite solidly and independently on its own very well articulated doctrinal foundations.

   Although Vasubandhu's treatise does seem to quote from a sutra or sutras (particularly in the last chapter, but also, perhaps, in those passages commencing with "Sons of the Buddha," etc.), Tripiṭaka Master Kumārajīva's translation nowhere preserves any of the usual text markers through which one might distinguish text from commentary. (It would be, by the way, highly unusual for Kumārajīva to fail to include such distinguishing language as "the Sutra states…," "the Commentary states…," etc., if indeed the text from which he was working contained any such delineating markers at all.) In short, sutra text(s) and treatise / commentary text are here more-or-less seamlessly interwoven.

   I felt as a consequence of the above factors that, in order to avoid unnecessary distortions of the text, I really had no choice but to translate into English just as Kumārajīva had done into Chinese, leaving any judgments on these secondary issues for the reader himself to contemplate. I dare say, I only defaulted to this position on the matter after experimenting over and over with a textual-analysis approach by which one might separate root text from commentary text. In every case, the number of passages which remained ambiguous as to their origin were so numerous that I eventually felt compelled to abandon the exercise as fruitless, unwise, and also useless: as it stands, the text is an eloquent and complete treatment of the subject and I see no reason to damage the text through well-meant but ill-advised editorial interventions. Perhaps we will eventually locate a root text somewhere in the vast Chinese Mahāyāna canon..
3. *Mahāvaipulya* is a reference to a category of "greatly expansive" teachings common to the entire Mahāyāna tradition.

4. Generally speaking, a *mātṛkā* is a treatise or essay which expands upon the basic meaning of a more straightforward idea or text. It functions to develop wisdom in the reader and is explained as meaning "mother of wisdom."
5. First, one may care to note that this first topic listed is the main subject of Chapter One whereas the eleven topics listed immediately after serve as the main subjects of Chapters Two through Twelve. (Four through Nine clearly represent the six perfections in their standard order.) The numbering here is inserted into the English edition to precisely reflect the numbered chapters of the Chinese edition.

   Second, one should realize that "unsurpassed bodhi" refers specifically and exclusively to the unsurpassed, right, and perfect enlightenment of a fully-realized buddha as distinct from the limited enlightenment of arhats and pratyekabuddhas.
6. "Adornment" here may seem like an obscure concept, but in fact it is simply a reference to marvelous effects produced much later in one's karmic continuum as a direct result of cultivating good karmic causes earlier in the long path from common person to fully-enlightened buddha. In these sorts of contexts, those karmic causes lie in the cultivation of the prerequisite merit and wisdom which eventually produce the effect of the body of a buddha being "adorned" by the thirty-two marks and eighty subsidiary characteristics. Those karmic causes also produce the effect of a buddha's buddhaland being adorned by many varied and perfect excellences. Where we see related phrases such as "adorning the path to bodhi" or "adorning the buddhaland," this generally refers to extraordinary skillfulness in cultivating spiritually potent altruistic bodhisattva practices.
7. This is a reference to the special "summit" mark (*uṣṇīṣa*) on the crown of a buddha's head. It is possessed only by buddhas and is such as, at least on the level of one's aura, no matter how high above a buddha one might search, one can never succeed in finding the highest point to which it reaches. On the physical level, it is manifest as a small prominence on the crown of a buddha's head.
8. In the *Taisho* edition of the text, the third and fourth of these topic listings are reversed when compared with the order of their relatively lengthy discussions which follow a few paragraphs later in the text. I therefore emend the text to switch the listing order of number three and number four so as to re-establish sequence consistency between the initial listings and the subsequent discussions.
9. The three stations of mindfulness for a buddha refer to his indifference to the circumstance where his disciples accept his teachings, to the circumstance where his disciples do not accept his teachings, and to the circumstance where some disciples do and some do not accept his teachings.

10. The four "currents" (*catur-ogha*) are desire, existence, ignorance, and views.
11. "The ground of dry wisdom" is the first in a schema of ten grounds not necessarily exclusive to the Bodhisattva Path. This particular station is so named because whilst still on that ground the practitioner's wisdom associated with contemplation has not yet been "moistened" by the "waters" of extremely deep meditative realization.
12. "Signless" giving would be that wherein one does not seize on the existence of a benefactor, recipient, or gift, this because one perceives all three to be devoid of any inherent existence and devoid of any truly-existent differentiating characteristics warranting the perception: "I am a benefactor, so-and-so is the recipient, and this is my gift."
13. The basic precepts most commonly taken up by the householder do not require celibacy, but do require refraining from "sexual misconduct." In those rare cases where a householder wishes to elevate the level of his practice to include strict celibacy, that is available as an option in the eight-precept moral code for the laity (*upavāsa*). Those eight precepts which require strict celibacy of the householder can be taken for just a single day, as a regimen wherein they are observed on six set days each lunar month, or for a two-week period from the first to the fifteenth of the twelfth lunar month. There is also probably no particular reason they couldn't be taken for any other set period of time (say, for a year or two of intensive cultivation), so long as the time was arranged in advance with the precept-transmitting monk.
14. "Three wretched destinies" refers to rebirth in the hell realms, ghost realms, or animal realms. As Ding Fubao's dictionary has it, the "Eight difficulties" refers to: 1) rebirth in the hells; 2) among ghosts; 3) among animals; 4) in Uttarakuru (a land where everything is blissful); 5) in the long-life heavens, blissful and seemingly secure locations in the form-realm and formless realm (these all are so enjoyable, one has no motivation to pursue the Path); 6) as deaf, blind or mute; 7) as endowed only with worldly intelligence and eloquence (through which one disdains and condescends to the idea of cultivating the Path); and 8) rebirth either before or after the appearance of a Buddha in the world.
15. Of the seven types of arrogance, one notices only five listed here. The two not mentioned are "arrogance in inferiority" (*adhamo māna*) and "perverse arrogance" (*mithyā-māna*).
16. "Brahmin conduct" is an explicit reference to celibacy, but also includes by direct implication abstention from killing, stealing, lying, and consumption of any form of intoxicant.

17. "Great adornment" is a reference to the bodhisattva's countless lifetimes of work devoted to the liberation of other beings. His selfless labors inevitably involve the production of an incalculably vast store of merit which manifests eventually in a fabulously refined pureland wherein that bodhisattva dwells once he gains complete realization of buddhahood. The bodhisattva's works in service to other beings create the marvelous adornment of his own pureland while also contributing to the adornment of the purelands of other buddhas through the presence in those buddha's assemblies of beings which he has brought to liberation.
18. In addition to the four components of the first dhyāna contained in quotation marks, there is an additional fifth component of the first dhyāna not mentioned here by Vasubandhu: "single-mindedness" (*citta-eka-agratā*).
19. I emend the text here to correct a clear scribal error by replacing *Taisho's shuo* (說) with the graphically similar *de* (得). An equally defensible emendation choice might perhaps be the phonically-similar *shou* (受) The text makes no sense as preserved in *Taisho*. As emended, the text accords with Vasubandhu's other writings and with other standard descriptions of this component of the third dhyāna.
20. If this clause on perceiving the nirvāṇa-like nature of all which a bodhisattva has labored to adorn seems obscure, refer to the note on "great adornment" several notes above.
21. An *araṇya* is a serene and secluded dwelling intended for solitary meditation.
22. *Vaipulya* means "expansive."
23. This is probably a reference to the eighth bodhisattva ground, the "ground of immovability" (*acala-bhūmi*), wherein:
One never emerges from the contemplation of ultimate truth;
The complete absence of mental discriminations is inconceivable;
One's level of realization is not such as would lie within the common person's sphere of body, mouth, or mind;
One's cultivation of the *pāramitā* of vows is constantly foremost;
One's realization is never reached by Two-Vehicles' practitioners;
Ultimate truth and worldly truth are of a single meaning; and
Through complete cultivation in both movement and stillness,
    one carries on endlessly the two types of benefit (self, other).

(The above is my paraphrase of verses 65-7 of Ārya Nāgārjuna's *Ratnāvalī*, Ch. 5.)

Variant Readings from Other Chinese Editions

Fascicle One Variant Readings

[p508n01] 〔經〕－【宋】【元】【明】【宮】＊
[p508n02] 〔天親菩薩造〕－【宮】＊
[p508n03] 後秦龜茲國三藏＝姚秦三藏法師【宋】＊【元】＊【明】＊，＝姚秦三藏【宮】＊
[p508n04] 忍＋（辱）【宋】【元】【明】【宮】
[p508n05] 礙＝癡【宋】【元】【明】【宮】＊［＊１２］
[p508n06] （法）＋門【宋】【元】【明】【宮】
[p508n07] （弟）＋子【宋】【元】【明】【宮】
[p509n01] 諸佛菩薩＝菩薩諸佛【宋】【元】【明】【宮】
[p509n02] 之＝大【元】【明】
[p509n03] 無邊無量＝無量無邊【宋】【元】【明】【宮】
[p509n04] （微）＋塵【宋】【元】【明】【宮】
[p509n05] 渧＝滴【宮】
[p509n06] 得受行＝使得聞【宋】【元】【明】【宮】
[p509n07] 〔發菩提心經論〕－【明】＊
[p509n08] 〔經〕－【宋】【元】【宮】＊［＊１２３４５］
[p509n09] 勝＝正【宋】【元】【明】【宮】
[p509n10] 修集＝修習【宋】【元】【明】【宮】下同
[p509n11] 〔中〕－【宋】【元】【明】【宮】
[p509n12] 道＝導【宋】【元】【明】【宮】
[p510n01] 惱苦＝苦惱【宋】【元】【明】【宮】
[p510n02] 燃＝然【宋】【元】【明】【宮】
[p510n03] （一者）＋願【宋】【元】【明】【宮】
[p510n04] 繫＝係【宮】
[p510n05] （二者）＋願【宋】【元】【明】【宮】
[p510n06] 〔永必〕－【宋】【元】【明】【宮】
[p510n07] （三者）＋願【宋】【元】【明】【宮】
[p510n08] （四者）＋願【宋】【元】【明】【宮】
[p510n09] （五者）＋願【宋】【元】【明】【宮】
[p510n10] 〔能〕－【宋】【元】【明】【宮】
[p510n11] （六者）＋願【宋】【元】【明】【宮】
[p510n12] （七者）＋願【宋】【元】【明】【宮】
[p510n13] （八者）＋願【宋】【元】【明】【宮】
[p510n14] （九者）＋願【宋】【元】【明】【宮】
[p510n15] （十者）＋願【宋】【元】【明】【宮】
[p510n16] 負荷＝荷負【宋】【元】【明】【宮】

[p510n17] 生＋（界）【宋】【元】【明】【宮】＊［＊1］
[p510n18] 菩薩善自＝自己【宋】【元】【明】【宮】
[p510n19] 應不＝不應【宋】【元】【明】【宮】
[p510n20] 欺＋（誑）【宋】【元】【明】【宮】＊［＊1］
[p511n01] 要＋（必）【宋】【元】【明】【宮】
[p511n02] 檀＋（那）【宋】【元】【明】【宮】
[p511n03] 他利＝利他【宋】【元】【明】【宮】
[p511n04] 令＝今【明】
[p511n05] 搏＝團【宋】【元】【明】【宮】
[p511n06] 綎＝線【宋】【元】【明】【宮】
[p511n07] 〔復〕－【宋】【元】【明】【宮】
[p511n08] 罝＝罩【宮】
[p511n09] 杖＝仗【宋】【元】【明】【宮】
[p511n10] 時＋（歡喜）【宋】【元】【明】【宮】
[p511n11] 具＋（足）【宋】【元】【明】【宮】
[p511n12] 檀＋（那）【宋】【元】【明】【宮】
[p511n13] 漏盡＝盡漏【宋】【元】【明】【宮】
[p512n01] 收＝守【宋】【元】【明】【宮】
[p512n02] 危＝厄【宋】【元】【明】【宮】
[p512n03] 歡＝勸【宋】【元】【明】【宮】
[p512n04] 支＝枝【宋】【元】【明】【宮】
[p512n05] 遠＝邊【宋】
[p512n06] 想＝相【宋】【元】【明】【宮】＊［＊1］
[p512n07] 濡＝軟【宋】【元】【明】【宮】＊
[p512n08] 大忍＝忍辱【宋】【元】【明】【宮】
[p512n09] 危＝威【宋】【元】【明】【宮】
[p512n10] 見＝有【宋】【元】【明】【宮】
[p512n11] 濡＝軟【宮】
[p512n12] 罪過＝過惡【宋】【元】【明】【宮】
[p512n13] 慊＝嫌【宋】【元】【明】【宮】
[p512n14] 常＝當【宋】【元】【明】【宮】
[p512n15] 猗＝倚【宋】【元】【明】【宮】＊［＊1 2］
[p513n01] （盡）＋結【宋】【元】【明】【宮】
[p513n02] （和）＋合【宋】【元】【明】【宮】
[p513n03] 忍＋（時）【宋】【元】【明】【宮】

Fascicle Two Variant Readings
[p513n04] 修集＝修習【宋】【元】【明】【宮】下同
[p513n05] 起＝生【宋】【元】【明】【宮】
[p513n06] 精進＝精勤【宋】【元】【明】【宮】
[p513n07] 起＝趣【宋】【元】【明】【宮】

Variant Readings in Other Editions

[p513n08] 諸佛＝佛諸【宋】【元】【明】【宮】
[p513n09] 〔發菩提心經論〕－【明】＊
[p513n10] 〔經〕－【宋】【元】【宮】＊［＊ 1 2 3 4］
[p513n11] 〔那〕－【宋】【元】【明】【宮】
[p513n12] 頂＝項【宋】【元】【明】【宮】
[p514n01] 自＝因【宮】
[p514n02] 邊＝有【宋】【元】【明】【宮】
[p514n03] 〔那〕－【宋】【元】【明】【宮】
[p514n04] 蜜＝密【宮】
[p514n05] 慧故＝智慧【宋】【元】【明】【宮】
[p514n06] 正道邪道＝邪道正道【宋】【元】【明】【宮】
[p515n01] 殖＝植【宋】【元】【明】【宮】
[p515n02] 善精進＝善根精勤【宋】【元】【明】【宮】
[p515n03] 〔化〕－【宋】【元】【明】【宮】
[p515n04] 厄＝危【宋】【元】【明】
[p515n05] 〔故〕－【宋】【元】【明】【宮】
[p516n01] 斑＝班【宋】【宮】，＝頒【元】【明】
[p516n02] 〔念亦空是名為空空〕－【宋】【元】【明】【宮】
[p516n03] 如＝以【宋】【元】【明】【宮】
[p516n04] 授＝受【宋】【元】【明】【宮】＊［＊ 1 2 3 4］
[p516n05] 菩薩＝有人【宋】【元】【明】【宮】
[p516n06] 以＝已【宋】【元】【明】【宮】
[p516n07] 如＝知【宮】
[p516n08] 取相＝妄想【宋】【元】【明】【宮】
[p516n09] 曾＝嘗【宋】【元】【明】【宮】
[p517n01] 其發＝發其【宋】【元】【明】【宮】
[p517n02] 令＝使【宋】【元】【明】【宮】
[p517n03] 已＝以【宋】【元】【明】【宮】
[p517n04] 報＝德【宋】【元】【明】【宮】
[p517n05] 〔經〕－【宋】【元】【明】【宮】

About the Translator

Bhikshu Dharmamitra (ordination name "Heng Shou"– 釋恆授) is a Chinese-tradition translator-monk and one of the early American disciples (since 1968) of the late Weiyang Ch'an patriarch, Dharma teacher, and exegete, the Venerable Master Hsuan Hua (宣化上人). He has a total of 23 years in robes during two periods as a monastic (1969–1975; 1991 to present).

Dharmamitra's principal educational foundations as a translator lie in four years of intensive monastic training and Chinese-language study of classic Mahāyāna texts in a small-group setting under Master Hua from 1968–1972, undergraduate Chinese language study at Portland State University, a year of intensive one-on-one Classical Chinese study at the Fu Jen University Language Center near Taipei, and two years at the University of Washington's School of Asian Languages and Literature (1988–90).

Since taking robes again under Master Hua in 1991, Dharmamitra has devoted his energies primarily to study and translation of classic Mahāyāna texts with a special interest in works by Ārya Nāgārjuna and related authors. To date, he has translated a dozen important texts, most of which are slated for publication by Kalavinka Press.

Kalavinka Buddhist Classics Title List

Meditation Instruction Texts

The Essentials of Buddhist Meditation
A marvelously complete classic *śamathā-vipaśyanā* (calming-and-insight) meditation manual. By Tiantai Śramaṇa Zhiyi (538–597 CE).

Six Gates to the Sublime
The earliest Indian Buddhist meditation method explaining the essentials of breath and calming-and-insight meditation. By Śramaṇa Zhiyi.

Bodhisattva Path Texts

Nāgārjuna on the Six Perfections
Chapters 17–30 of Ārya Nāgārjuna's *Mahāprajñāpāramitā Upadeśa*.

Marvelous Stories from the Perfection of Wisdom
130 stories from Ārya Nāgārjuna's *Mahāprajñāpāramitā Upadeśa*.

A Strand of Dharma Jewels (Ārya Nāgārjuna's *Ratnāvalī*)
The earliest extant edition, translated by Paramārtha: ca 550 CE

Nāgārjuna's Guide to the Bodhisattva Path
The *Bodhisaṃbhāra Treatise* with abridged Vaśitva commentary.

The Bodhisaṃbhāra Treatise Commentary
The complete exegesis by the Indian Bhikshu Vaśitva (*ca* 300–500 CE).

Letter from a Friend - The Three Earliest Editions
The earliest extant editions of Ārya Nāgārjuna's *Suhṛlekkha*:
Translated by Tripiṭaka Master Guṇavarman (*ca* 425 CE)
Translated by Tripiṭaka Master Saṅghavarman (*ca* 450 CE)
Translated by Tripiṭaka Master Yijing (*ca* 675 CE)

Resolve-for-Enlightenment Texts

On Generating the Resolve to Become a Buddha
On the Resolve to Become a Buddha by Ārya Nāgārjuna
Exhortation to Resolve on Buddhahood by Patriarch Sheng'an Shixian
Exhortation to Resolve on Buddhahood by the Tang Literatus, Peixiu

Vasubandhu's Treatise on the Bodhisattva Vow
By Vasubandhu Bodhisattva (*ca* 300 CE)

*All Kalavinka Press translations include facing-page source text.

www.ingramcontent.com/pod-product-compliance
Lightning Source LLC
LaVergne TN
LVHW011421080426
835512LV00005B/201